GOOD COOKING with
NATURAL FOODS

Lorie & Don

Happy cooking to
people who enjoy
the "Art of Eating"!

Muriel

SELF-PORTRAIT SKETCH BY ROBERT POPE (1956-1992)

"Robert Pope was an outstanding artist,
a remarkable human being, a wonderful friend and the
backbone of the macrobiotic community in Halifax, NS.
He lives on in his works, and in the hearts of all who knew him."
- MURIEL VIBERT

GOOD COOKING with NATURAL FOODS

by
Muriel Vibert

LANCELOT
PRESS

ISBN 0-88999-600-8
Published 1996

Illustrations: F.M. Rose

LANCELOT PRESS LIMITED, Hantsport, Nova Scotia.
Office and production facilities situated on Highway No. 1,
1/2 mile east of Hantsport.

MAILING ADDRESS:
P.O. Box 425, Hantsport, N.S. B0P 1P0

*This book is dedicated to my
grandmother and mother,
who cooked the simple way.*

Acknowledgements

Special thanks to:

Diane Silver-Hassell and **Dr Chris Hassell**,
Toronto, Ontario
My first macrobiotic counsellors.

Wayne Diotte, senior macrobiotic counsellor,
founder/director of Macrobiotics Canada,
in Almonte, Ontario   (613) 256-2665.
My counsellor, teacher and friend since 1984.

Barbara Jannasch, teacher, counsellor,
founder of Akala Point Retreat,
Indian Harbour, Nova Scotias   (902) 823-2160
Thanks for the "haven", Barbara.

Family and friends *who didn't throw me out
with the dish water just because I was
doing something different.*

Contents

Foreword

Macrobiotics is a way of approaching life. It offers a large view, a way of perceiving, pursuing, creating and living. A Great Life — full of energy, good humor and adventure.

Understanding and balancing the energy of our daily food, relationships, environment and activities is an enjoyable and rewarding focus of macrobiotics.

The philosophical roots of macrobiotics can be traced to the ancient wisdom of peace-loving people throughout the world. Its essence is universally understandable and as such may be enjoyed and used by anyone, anytime, anyplace. As with all learning, leadership and health discipline study, practice accelerates one's progress.

Daily food is a cornerstone of living a great life. Diet and cooking have a profound and powerful influence on creating our overall health. This influence manifests itself in the quality of our blood and thereby our mental and emotional well-being. Of course being healthy, balanced and energetic affords us the opportunity to grow spiritually according to our heart's desire.

Hippocrates, who is considered the founding father of modern medicine, said, "Let food be thy medicine and medicine be thy food." This common sense principle is at the heart of macrobiotic understanding and when combined with a spirit of love, contributes to creating a world full of health, happiness and peace.

As a counsellor, Muriel Vibert has inspired me with the quality of her questions and her will to take result-oriented actions.

As an educator, I am grateful for Muriel's consistent, thorough and loving contribution to many of my clients and students. Muriel was an integral part of a flourishing Macrobiotics East Group and presently, as president of The Vancouver Macrobiotic Society, she continues her tradition of hands-on involvement with macrobiotics in Canada.

Observing and participating in Muriel's growth and many changes, she has prompted me to live with courage to express my own inner greatness, as I embrace a world community that is more than ever open to the great art/ science/philosophy we call macrobiotics.

Good Cooking with Natural Foods takes you on a delightful journey of tastes and textures. You will find some of them so familiar it's like being in your parents' or grandparents' kitchen, and yet there is always this sense of goodness that goes well beyond delicious familiarity.

These recipes create nourishing food by integrating the finest quality natural foods with macrobiotic cooking and health principles.

All the practical hints, organizing methods, inspirational verses, good humour and sincerity in this book will serve you, your friends and family for many years. It is going into our 'Education That Lasts a Lifetime Library' and onto my 'excellent gifts' list.

Good Cooking with Natural Foods is destined to become an all-time favourite!

> *as we journey*
> > *through our Great Life*
> *may we be graced with*
> > *remembrance …*
> *every now is*
> > *perfect*
> *let it change*
> > *let it change.*

WAYNE DIOTTE
Founder/Director,
Macrobiotics Canada
Almonte, Ontario

Introduction

The idea for this book started at a cooking session at my house. In the midst of instructing 10 people crowded in an 18-tile kitchen, Mike quietly said: "I think Muriel should write a cookbook."

All agreed it was a good idea — except me. I don't follow recipes. I have hypoglycemia as well as many food allergies and my cooking was based on what I could eat. I also like to add a bit of this, try a bit of that, and forget about measuring anything. To make it different every time is an easy way to cook, but is this the way to write a cookbook? Leona, another friend, requested that I include "thoughts".

These friends have been very patient with me, and now I have put together many recipes and "thoughts" that I hope will be enjoyed and bring health. Many recipes in this book are basic macrobiotic while some bridge the gap mixing old and new ingredients for good taste and better nutrition.

Macrobiotics has played a very large role in my road back to good health. It has been a wonderful experience with new foods and new friends. Before macrobiotics, the emphasis was on what I couldn't eat, but now I think about all the new tasty foods I can eat.

After my health improved, I began to experiment with some of my old favourite foods. Fish cakes, fish loaf and tourtière again became part of my diet, but this time with different ingredients. My hope is that these recipes will encourage others not to give up their favourite dishes — instead, to experiment and change them to suit their own needs and tastes.

Cooking is mainly learning the basics and then combining the basic rules in various ways. If the dish turns out well but not in the way you expected, you can always give it a different name.

What also made macrobiotics very special was the people I met: the members of the Macrobiotic East Group and Macrobiotics Vancouver, the customers at Mrs Murphy's Kitchen, and at The Olive Tree, the new friends that were very supportive of one another; and the fun we had at cooking classes, the "do nothing, get away weekends" at Akala Point and The Ovens, and those wonderful potlucks. Who says changing your diet means giving up — for me it was a wonderful new beginning.

Getting Started Shopping Guide

GRAINS
Short grain brown rice
Barley
Oats
Millet
Sweet brown rice
Rolled oats
Noodles

BEANS & BEAN PRODUCTS
Aduki beans
Lentils
Chick peas
Black soybeans
Tempeh
Tofu

SEA VEGETABLES (VEGS)
Nori
Arame
Hijiki
Kombu
Wakame
Dulse

SEASONINGS
Sea Salt
Tamari
Barley miso
Umeboshi Vinegar
Fresh ginger root

VEGETABLES
Carrots
Turnips
Parsnips
Daikon
Squash
Cauliflower
Kale
Broccoli
Watercress
Scallions
Onions
Chinese cabbage
Bok choy
Parsley
Burdock — fresh or dried

Whole grains, beans, sea vegs and seasonings can be purchased in bulk.
Root vegetables can be purchased in bulk if you have good storage.
Greens you should buy fresh in small quantities. The produce manager in your grocery store can tell you which day the fresh greens come in.
Parsley can be grown indoors during the winter.

Conversions

Reducing a large recipe into one for two or three servings can sometimes be difficult. I find the easiest way is to convert the original amounts to millilitres, reduce the recipe to the desired size and then work in millilitres or change it back to cup and spoon measure.

Spoons to millilitres (ml)

1/8 tsp	=	.6 ml
1/4 tsp	=	1.2 ml
1/2 tsp	=	2.5 ml
1 tsp	=	5.0 ml
1/2 tbsp	=	7.5 ml
1 tbsp	=	15.0 ml
1 tbsp	= 3 tsp	= 15 ml

Cups/	millilitres/	Spoons
1/8	30	2 tbsp
1/4	60	4 tbsp
1/3	80	5 tbsp + 1 tsp
3/8	90	6 tbsp
1/2	125	8 tbsp + 1 tsp
2/3	160	10 tbsp + 2 tsp
3/4	180	12 tbsp
1	250	16 tbsp + 2 tsp
2	500	33 tbsp + 1 tsp

Substitutes

SALT / TAMARI / UMEBOSHI VINEGAR / MISO

1 pinch sea salt	=	1/2 tsp tamari
	=	1/2 tsp umeboshi vinegar
	=	2/3 tsp miso
1/8 tsp sea salt	=	3/4 tsp tamari
	=	3/4 tsp umeboshi vinegar
	=	generous 3/4 tsp miso
1/4 tsp sea salt	=	1 1/2 tsp tamari
	=	1 1/2 tsp umeboshi vinegar
	=	1 2/3 tsp miso
1 umeboshi plum	=	1/4 tsp sea salt
	=	1 1/2 tsp tamari
	=	1 2/3 tsp miso
	=	1 1/2 tsp umeboshi vinegar
	=	1 1/2 tsp umeboshi paste

I sometimes use miso in place of salt in baking (this helps the rising action) and vinegar in pie crusts.

EGGS

My favourite substitute for eggs is tahini.
1 tbsp tahini + 3 tbsp liquid = 1 egg or
1 tbsp arrowroot flour + 3 tbsp liquid = 1 egg

KUZU / ARROWROOT FLOUR

1 tbsp kuzu = 3 tbsp arrowroot flour
To thicken 1 cup liquid use approximately 1 tbsp kuzu or 3 tbsp arrowroot flour. Dissolve kuzu in cold water.

Soup

One or two small bowls per day.
Light soup for breakfast or before the main meal.
*A heartier soup including grains and beans may be served with a light meal, **or** as the meal.*
Stimulates the appetite.

Soup is made up of
sea vegetables
2 or 3 vegetabless (I always include onions)
water or stock
miso, tamari or salt
garnish
Heartier soups may also contain beans, grains or fish.

Sea Vegs used in soup
kombu, wakame, kelp and dulse
rich in minerals and vitamins

Onion
gives soup sweet flavour when well cooked.

Carrots and squash
also give the soup a sweet taste.

Daikon
white radish also called lobok. Daikon aids digestion and helps
to break down and eliminate animal fats and excess water from
the body. Use daikon in moderation.

Miso
is a fermented product made from soybeans, salt and barley,
rice, millet, chickpeas, etc. For daily use, I prefer 2-year
unpasturized barley miso. Miso is rich in living enzymes and is
very good for digestion. It is very strengthening and creates
energy — fresh garnish helps to utilize that energy. Miso is very
tasty but also salty and therefore it is best not to use too much
— 1/2 to 1 tsp of miso per cup of liquid. Too much salt will
cause a craving for sweets, and constant hunger.

Tamari
is a natural soy sauce, made from soybeans, water, wheat and
sea salt. Wheat-free is available; tamari does not contain sugar
or other sweetners, and low sodium tamari may contain alcohol
(read labels). Very delicious and it's easy to use too much — like
miso, it is salty so use with awareness.

Light Miso Soup

4 cups water
1 three inch piece of kombu
1 small onion
1 medium carrot
1 inch piece daikon
2-4 tsp miso
parsley to garnish

Put 4 cups of water in the soup pot.
Break the kombu into very small pieces, rinse in cold water to remove the dirt and excess salt, and add to the soup pot. Bring to boil.
Slice onion very thin, add to the soup, turn the heat down and cook at a gentle simmer for 5 minutes.
Slice daikon paper thin, add to the soup and cook for about 10 minutes.
Slice carrot paper thin, add to the soup and cook for another 5 minutes.
Purée the miso with soup water in a suribachi or small bowl, add to the soup and simmer 5 minutes.
Garnish with parsley.

Servings 4 to 5
Prep time 10 - 15 minutes   *Cooking time 20 - 30 minutes*

Variations
- Vary the cooking time for softer or crisper vegetables.
- Try other sea vegetables, i.e kombu, kelp or dulse.
- Use other vegetables.

A very important part of soup is the cook's Tender Loving Care.

Veggie Miso Soup

4 cups water   1/4 cup cauliflower
3" strip wakame   1/4 cup broccoli
1 small onion   1 - 2 tsp miso
1 small carrot   parsley for garnish
1/2 corn (in season)

Wipe wakame, then soak and cut in 1" squares.
Cut onions and carrots in 1/4" cubes.
Cut corn off the cob (boil the cob in the soup water and remove
before adding the miso).
Cut cauliflower and broccoli into small pieces.

Add wakame and corn cob to the water and cook 10 minutes.
Add onions, carrots and corn and cook gently for 10 minutes.
Add cauliflower and broccoli stems and cook 5 minutes.
Remove the corn cob.
Add broccoli.
Purée the miso with soup water, add to the soup and simmer
3 to 5 minutes.
Garnish with parsley before serving.

Servings 4
Preparation time 15 minutes   Cooking time 30 minutes

Variations
- Shorter cooking time will keep the vegetables crisper. In cold
  weather I like the vegs cooked soft but in hot weather I prefer
  them a bit on the crisp side.

Time spent in lovingly preparing food is an investment.

Watercress Miso Soup

4 cups water
3" piece of kombu
1/2 small onion
1/2 cup watercress
1 - 2 tsp miso

Wipe kombu, place in water and bring to boil.
Gently simmer for 10 minutes and remove. (The kombu may be used in another recipe).
Cut onion in paper-thin slices, add to soup and simmer for 5 minutes.
Separate watercress leaves from the stems.
Cut stems in small pieces
Add stems and leaves to soup. Purée miso with soup water and add to soup. Simmer 3 minutes.

Servings 4
Preparation time 5 minutes   Cooking time 20 minutes

Variations
- Cooking water from corn, carrots or squash adds a nice flavour and colour.
- Grated carrots can be added to soup at the same time as the watercress.
- 3 blanched carrot flowers added to the soup bowl make this very attractive.

Nurture ourselves — body, mind and soul.
To care for only our body is like trying to
live on only one meal a day.

Ginger Tamari Broth

4 cups water or carrot cooking water
3" strip of kombu
1 small onion
1 medium carrot
2 - 4 tsp tamari
1 - 1 1/2 tsp freshly grated ginger juice
Scallions to garnish

Wash kombu, place in soup pot with 1 cup of water and onion. Bring to boil, reduce heat and simmer for 5 minutes. Remove onion and kombu. The kombu may be used in another dish. Add 3 cups of water or carrot cooking water.*
Cut the carrot into thin flowers, add to the soup and simmer 3 minutes.
Grate the ginger and squeeze out the juice. Add the ginger juice and tamari to the soup and simmer 5 minutes. **
Garnish with scallions.

Servings 8 (1/2 cup per serving)
Preparation time 10 minutes   *Cooking time 10 minutes*

Variations
- Cooking the onion for a longer time will give the soup a sweeter taste

* Leftover vegetables can become acidic, therefore I prefer using the cooking water from the same meal to make the soup.
** Add ginger near the end of the cooking as it can go bitter if it is added too soon.

Improve the quality of food to improve the quality of life.

Dulse-Squash Miso Soup

4 cups water
1 small onion
1/2 small squash
1/4 cup dulse
2 - 4 tsp miso
Scallions

Slice onion thin.
Peel squash and cut in small cubes.
Tear dulse in small pieces and rinse in cold water.
Cook onions, squash and dulse in 2 cups water for about
15 minutes, at a gentle boil.
Mash squash, add 2 more cups of water and cook for
5 minutes.
Purée the miso with soup water and add to soup.
Simmer 3 - 5 minutes.
Garnish with scallions.

Servings 4
Preparation time 10 minutes   Cooking time 30 minutes

Variations
- Kombu, kelp or wakame may be used instead of dulse.
- The peel may be left on organic squash but the soup will be
  more greenish than orange.

I am grateful for the gift of this beautiful day.
I will use it wisely and experience every moment.
At day's end I will rejoice knowing I did my best.

Split Pea Soup

3 - 4 cups water
1/4 cup dulse
1/2 small squash
1/2 cup split peas

1 small onion
2 - 4 tsp miso or tamari
Parsley for garnish

Rinse the dulse in cold water.
Peel and cube the squash.
Cut the onion in small pieces.

In pressure cooker, layer the dulse, onions, split peas and squash. Add water. Cover pressure cooker, bring to high pressure. Turn heat down very low and cook 5 - 10 minutes. Remove from heat and let pressure come down slowly. Return soup to low heat and cook uncovered until peas are soft. Purée miso with the soup water, add to soup and simmer 5 minutes.

Garnish with parsley just before serving.

Variations
- Adjust the amount of water for desired consistency.
- Split peas do not have to be soaked. However, like most beans, they are easier to digest if soaked.
- Can also be cooked in soup pot — allow about 1 hour.
- Do not leave pressure cooker unattended as split peas can block the valve. If this happens remove from heat and let the pressure come down slowly.

Servings 3 - 4
Preparation time 10 minutes   Cooking time 30 minutes

I like serving this on dull, cold days as the colour is very cheery and the soup is warming.

You are what you eat.

Squash-Aduki Bean Soup

4 cups water
1 small onion
1/2 cup squash
2 tbsp cooked arame

4 tbsp cooked aduki beans
2 - 3 tsp miso
scallions to garnish

Slice onions very thin.
Cut squash about 1/8 inch thick and 1/2 inch square.
Cook onions and squash in 2 cups of water about 10 minutes at a gentle boil. Add arame, aduki beans and 2 cups water (vegetable cooking water may be used) and cook for another 5 minutes.
Purée the miso with soup water, add to the soup and simmer over low heat for 5 minutes.
Garnish with scallions.

Servings 4
Preparation time 10 minutes   Cooking time 20 minutes

Variations
- More aduki beans may be added for a heartier soup.
- More squash may be used. For a creamier soup purée the squash.
- Cooked squash can also be used.
- When using cooked foods which have already been seasoned, taste the soup before adding the miso and adjust accordingly.

Gratitude is an important part of healing and of living.
Give yourself a few minutes each day
*   to feel grateful for who you are*
and all the wonderful people you know.

Grains

Complex carbohydrates.
Source of food energy.
Rich in fiber.
50% to 60% of our diet.

Brown rice
Use daily — easy to digest.
Short grain for short days.
Long grain for long days (hot, summer days).
Pressure cooking makes the rice easier to digest and promotes healing.

Millet
More akaline, it is great for an acidic stomach, spleen and pancreas. It creates warmth so it is a good winter food, and an important grain for anyone with a sugar problem.

Barley
Very soothing food. Barley added to soup creates a very peaceful feeling. People with hypoglycemia like its calming effect.

Grain products include bread, noodles and seitan.
Seitan is made from wheat gluten. It is very rich in protein.

Grains can be cooked alone or in combination with other grains and vegetables.

A pinch of salt per cup of grain brings out the flavour and adds to the energy.

Grains should be well cooked to make them easier to digest.

Soaking also makes grains easier to cook and digest.

Dry roasting gives grains a rich, nutty taste.

Brown Rice — Pressure Cooked

2 cups organic short grain brown rice
3 cups water (1 1/2 cups water to 1 cup rice)
2 pinches good quality sea salt

Wash rice, place in pressure cooker, add water and salt. Cover the pressure cooker and place on high heat. Bring to full pressure, turn heat down to very low and cook for 45 - 50 minutes. There should be just a gentle hiss from the pressure. Remove from heat and let the pressure come down slowly. This will take about 15 minutes. Leave the pressure cooker covered until ready to serve the rice.
Before serving the rice, stir from top to bottom to get a good yin-yang balance. (Dipping the wooden paddle in cold water prevents the rice from sticking to it.)

Servings 5 - 6
(1 cup of uncooked rice makes 2 1/2 to 3 servings)
Preparation time 5 minutes   Cooking time 60 minutes

Variations
- Bring to a boil and then cover the pressure cooker.
- Bring to high pressure on low heat (allow for the extra time).
- Use kombu instead of salt.
- Use shiso leaves instead of salt.
- For festive meals, substitute 1/4 cup of the brown rice with wild rice, country wild rice or wehani rice.
- Add arame and grated carrots to the rice before cooking.
- Add chopped parsley to the cooked rice just before serving.

There are no limits to the variations. Use your imagination, experiment, and have fun!

Cooking is a good way to practice unconditional love.
The little extras make the difference.

Brown Rice — Boiled

2 cups brown rice
2 pinches sea salt
4 cups water

Wash rice and place in pot with a tight fitting cover.
Add water and sea salt.
Cover and bring to boil.
Turn heat to low and cook for 1 hour and 5 minutes.
Fluff rice with wooden paddle, mixing the rice on top with the rice on the bottom.

Servings 5 - 6
Preparation time 5 minutes   Cooking time 1 hour 5 minutes

Variations
- Add more water for a softer rice.
- Add more water in very hot weather.

My favourite rice is Lundberg and I would like to give thanks to the Lundberg farmers for the loving energy they put into the growing of this wonderful grain.

Rice and Barley

1 cup short grain brown rice
1/4 cup barley
pinch sea salt
2 cups water

Wash and dry roast barley.
Wash rice.
Put barley and rice in pressure cooker and add water and salt.
Cover and bring to full pressure, lower heat and cook gently for 60 minutes.
Remove from heat and let pressure come down slowly.
Let sit in covered pressure cooker 15 minutes before serving.

Servings 3 - 4
Preparation time 15 minutes   Cooking time 65 minutes

Variations
- The rice also may be dry roasted.
- The barley could be soaked overnight.
- The barley and rice could be equal amounts.

Do not fear that by giving you will have to do without,
For that which you give comes back ten-fold,
And that which you withhold, will be withheld from you.

Brown Rice and Arame

2 cups short grain brown rice
1/4 cup arame
2 pinches sea salt
3 cups water

Wash and soak arame 5 minutes. Cut in 1/2 inch pieces.
Wash rice.
Put rice and arame in pressure cooker. Add water and salt.
Cover pressure cooker and bring to high pressure. Reduce heat
and cook at low pressure for 50 minutes.
Let pressure come down slowly.

Servings 4 - 6
Preparation time 10 minutes   Cooking time 50 minutes

The arame makes the rice quite dark. Therefore, it is important
that colorful vegetables are used in the meal.

*Sometimes when our prayers are answered it seems that we did
not get what we asked for. It is important to realize that our
prayers are based on our perception of where we are in our lives at
that moment — a limited view.*

   *The Divine has a limitless view and sees and knows all. The
answer therefore is based on not only where we are but also where
we can go, not only who we are at the moment but also all we can
become.*

Brown Rice and Black Soybeans

1 cup short grain brown rice
1/4 cup black soybeans
1/4 cup diced carrots
2 cups water
pinch sea salt
1/8 cup chopped parsley

Wash black soybeans by gently wiping with a damp towel.
Dry roast black soybeans in skillet over low heat until the skins
crack. Place in pressure cooker.
Wash rice and place in pressure cooker.
Dice carrots and place in pressure cooker.
Add a pinch of salt and 2 cups of water. Cover and bring to
high pressure. Reduce heat to low and gently cook for
65 minutes.
Remove from heat and let pressure come down slowly.

Add chopped parsley just before serving.

Servings 3 - 4
Preparation time 15 minutes   Cooking time 65 minutes

Variations
- Corn may be used, in season, in place of or in addition to the
  carrots.
- Black soybeans may be soaked overnight instead of roasting.
- Add salt to the soaking water to prevent the skins from
  coming off.

It's important to keep the kitchen neat and orderly.
If there's clutter in the kitchen
There's clutter in the food,
And clutter in your life.

Millet and Cauliflower

2 cups millet   6 - 7 cups water
1 small onion   3 pinches sea salt
1 cup cauliflower

Dice onion.
Cut cauliflower into small flowerettes.
Wash millet very well.

Layer onions, cauliflower and millet in pot.
Add salt and water.
Cover and bring to boil.
Reduce heat to low and simmer 30 minutes.
Mash, adding boiling water if too dry.

Servings 4 - 6
Preparation time 10 minutes   Cooking time 40 minutes

Variations
- Use the cooking water from carrots or squash when mashing
  the millet.
- Vegetables such as carrots, parsnips, and squash can be used
  along with the cauliflower or in place of the cauliflower.

Our feathered friends also enjoy the warmth of millet on a cold
winter's day.

Fluffy Millet

2 cups millet
4 cups water
2 pinches sea salt

Wash millet well and drain. Dry roast in skillet on medium to low heat until the grains are golden brown and release a nutty aroma. Stir constantly. This will take about 10 - 15 minutes but the results are worth it.
Add 4 cups boiling water, salt and bring to boil again. Cover skillet, reduce heat to low and gently simmer for 30 minutes.

Servings 4 - 6
Preparation time 20 minutes   Cooking time 35 minutes

Variations
- It will be fluffier if cooked spread out in a wide pan like a skillet rather than in a small pot.
- Use the cooking water from carrots or squash.
- Cook with a slice of ginger and remove before serving.
- Serve with a dish that has a sauce or gravy as the millet is very dry.
- Sprinkle finely chopped pickled ginger in the cooked millet.
- Use leftover millet in lentil burgers, tourtière, soup, etc.

A friend had this hanging in her kitchen and when I read it, it made me think about the members of the Macrobiotic East Group.

"Miss you?
        Well I guess I do.
Do I miss the sky when it ain't blue?
Do I miss the sun when it don't shine?
Or the blossoms gay
        when they droop 'n pine?
Miss you?
        Well, I guess I do —
Folks like you, are mighty few! "

Beans / Bean Products

Source of protein — needed for growth and repair.
5-10% of our diet.

Gas from beans is caused by
- overeating
- undercooking
- not chewing enough

Overeating beans can also cause a feeling of
tiredness. Cooking beans with kombu makes
them easier to digest. It's best to have beans at
lunch or supper in small amounts.

Aduki beans and rice
good for the kidneys and adrenals.

Aduki beans with squash and kombu
help the spleen, pancreas, stomach and digestion. They also
help to increase vitality.

Black soybeans
help to discharge animal toxins from the body. Soak or dry roast
before cooking. Do not pressure cook alone as the skins can
block the valve.

Soybeans
very rich in protein. Used mainly as miso, tofu and tempeh.
Tofu can be very cooling. Great in the summer but eat in
moderation.

Lentils
delicious in soups, stews, burgers or shepherd's pie. Does not
have to be soaked but soaking will make them easier to digest.

Ice bean (and Rice Dream) are good replacements for ice cream
but should be eaten in moderation.

Aduki Beans

3" piece of kombu   Water
1 onion   1-2 tsp tamari
1 cup aduki beans (soaked) parsley

Sort through beans and wash well. Soak overnight or 5 hours.
Wipe kombu to remove dust and excess salt and place in
bottom of pot.
Slice onion and place on top of kombu.
Add beans and water (just enough to cover the beans). Bring to
a boil, reduce heat and cook gently for 30 - 45 minutes. Add
cold water as needed to keep the top of the beans just covered.
When beans are 80% cooked add tamari and cook another
10-20 minutes, cooking most of the water off.
Garnish with parsley.

Servings 8 - 10
Preparation time 10 minutes   *Soaking time 5 hours to overnight*
Cooking time 1-1 1/2 hours

Variations
- Squash or carrots may be cooked with the beans for a sweeter
  taste.
- Excess water may be drained off and used in cooking brown
  rice.

Aduki beans are good food for the kidneys.

*Eating a lot of food and still starving? Check the amount of salt
you are eating. This also includes miso and tamari. A small
amount of good quality salt is important in the diet, however, too
much can be damaging to the kidneys, causing anger, irritability
and rigidity.*

Lentils — Boiled

2 inch piece of kombu
1 cup lentils
1 medium carrot

1 small onion
2 1/2 cups water
1- 2 tsp tamari

Carefully pick through the lentils to remove stones and then wash gently.

Break kombu into small pieces and wash in cold water. Place kombu in small pot.

Chop onion and place on top of kombu.

Cut carrot in slivers and place on top of onion.

Place lentils on top of carrot and onion.

Slowly add the water without disturbing the vegetables and lentils.

Bring to boil, reduce the heat and cook at a gentle simmer for about 40 minutes, adding more water if needed.

Add the tamari and cook for another 10 to 20 minutes.

Lentils should be well cooked, soft but not mushy.

Longer, slower cooking makes the lentils easier to digest and the flavour is sweeter.

Servings: 1 cup of uncooked lentils makes about 10 servings.
Preparation time 10 minutes   Cooking time 60 minutes

I am fortunate to live in such a beautiful country as Canada. When I travel from the Atlantic in the East to the Pacific in the West, I have many methods of travel to choose from.

I can quickly go to my destination by jet, or I can travel the fixed route of the train with many stops along the way, or I can travel by car, exploring many of the backroads. Granted, the backroads will have ruts and the travelling will be slower, but there I will see some of the most spectular scenery in our country.

Isn't life really a lot like that? *I can focus on reaching my goal and not pay much attention to the journey or I can experience it all — the ruts and mountain peaks, the barrens and the richness.*

Life is the great journey. The trail I travel is my choice.

Chick Peas

2" piece of kombu   1 cup chick peas (soaked)
1 small onion   3 cups water
1 medium carrot   1 - 2 tsp tamari

Pick over, wash and soak chick peas overnight.
Break kombu into small pieces, rinse and put in pressure cooker.
Dice onion and carrot and add to pressure cooker.
Drain chick peas and add to pressure cooker.
Add water, cover pressure cooker and bring to high pressure.
Lower heat and cook at low pressure for about 1 hour.
Remove from heat and allow pressure to come down slowly.
Add tamari and cook uncovered for about 15 minutes or until chick peas are completely cooked.

Servings 8 - 10
Soaking time overnight
Preparation time 5 minutes   Cooking time 1 1/2 - 2 hours

CHICK PEA TID BITS
- It is important to cook chick peas very well; if not they can be difficult to digest.
- To test, cut a chick pea in half. It is cooked when it is the same colour all the way through.
- Some people have trouble digesting the skins of the chick peas. After the peas have cooked, skim off the loose skins.
- I like my chick peas to have a sweet flavour so after I uncover the pressure cooker, I add the tamari and cook most of the water off. This makes the remaining liquid more like a sauce. For really sweet chick peas, I only pressure cook the peas for 45 minutes and then cook uncovered longer, cooking the water off and adding more cold water and cooking that off. I repeat this until the chick peas are cooked. It takes a bit of time but the results are worth it.

Split Peas

2" piece of kombu   water
1/2 small onion   1/2 - 1 tsp tamari
1 small carrot   parsley for garnish
1/2 cup split peas

Break kombu in small pieces, rinse and place in bottom of pot.
Cut onion and carrot into 1/4" cubes. Place on top of kombu.
Gently wash split peas and place on top of carrots.
Add water to about 1/2" over top of peas.
Bring to boil. Remove foam. Reduce heat to gentle boil and
cook approximately 50 minutes, adding cold water if necessary.
When almost cooked, add tamari and cook 10 minutes more.
Add parsley just before serving.

Servings 4
Preparation time 10 minutes   *Cooking time 60 minutes*

Variations
- Scallions may be used for garnish.
- Parsley may be chopped fine and added to peas in the last
  minute of cooking.

*Recently I read that only a dead palate needs spice, and while I
feel that this is a slight exaggeration it did remind me of a friend's
frank comment . This friend had decided, for reasons of health, to
try the macrobiotic diet. She was used to heavily seasoned food
and in macrobiotic cooking we use only light seasoning and very
little spices. After about her fourth or fifth meal she said "Is this
miso soup ever good, but I have to tell you the first time I ate your
soup, I said to my husband after, that woman doesn't waste
anything because I'm sure she used the dishwater today to make
the soup". We had many a good laugh about this after.*

*After we start eating macrobiotic foods it takes about four days
for our taste buds to adjust and then we start to enjoy the delicate
flavours of the grains and vegetables .*

Sweet and Sour Tempeh

1 small package tempeh   2 - 3 tsp tamari
1 onion   1 tsp umeboshi vinegar
1 carrot   1 tsp mirin
1 scallion   1/2 tsp grated ginger
1 tsp gomashio   1/2 - 1 cup water

Parboil tempeh with 1 tsp tamari and just enough water to cover the tempeh for 20 minutes or until all the water has been absorbed. Cut in cubes or thin slices.
Cut onion in thin half circles and water sauté with gomashio and 1 tsp tamari for 10 minutes.
Add tempeh and continue to saute.
Mix 1/2 cup water, 1 tsp tamari, 1 tsp umeboshi vinegar, and 1 tsp mirin. Add to tempeh and simmer 10 - 15 minutes, adding more water as necessary.
Cut carrot into small cubes, add to pan and simmer 10 minutes.
Add grated ginger and simmer 5 - 10 minutes.
Garnish with scallions.

Servings 4
Preparation time 10 minutes   *Cooking time 60 minutes*

Variations
- A small amount of oil can be used to sauté the onions and tempeh.
- For oil-free sautéeing, using a bit of tamari and gomashio enhances the flavour.

Always in a hurry — don't want to waste your time chewing your food?
What good does chewing actually do?
1. Relieves tension
2. Aids digestion. Some foods are digested in the mouth.
3. Releases the natural flavour of the food. The longer grains and vegetables are chewed the sweeter they become.

Scrambled Tofu

1/2 block tofu	1/4 to 1/2 cup water
2 onions	1/2 tsp umeboshi vinegar
2 small carrots	scallions or parsley
1 tbsp tamari	2 tsp gomashio
1 tsp tamari	

Mash tofu with fork. Add 1 tsp umeboshi vinegar and 1 tbsp tamari and marinate for about 30 minutes.
Sauté the onions in 1/4 cup water, 1 tsp tamari and 1 tsp gomashio for about 15 minutes. The longer the onions cook the sweeter the taste.
Cut the carrots into small cubes or sticks, add to the onions and cook about 5 minutes.
Add tofu and cook for 5 minutes. Stir and cook another 5 minutes. Finely chop the scallions or parsley fine and add in the last minute of cooking.

Servings 4
Preparation time 35 minutes   *Cooking time 30 minutes*

Variations
- For a drier dish press the tofu ahead of time to remove the water.
- For a creamier consistency add more water during cooking.
- Purée cooked carrots added to the scrambled tofu make a nice sauce.

The grass is always greener on the other side of the fence. This is quite often true when that fence is our own self-imposed limitations.

While this is one of the hardest fences to remove or break down, it only takes a very small gate to make a way to the other side.

Tofu Cheese — Homemade

1/2 lb firm tofu
miso

Cut tofu into 1/2" slices. Press 1 hour to remove water.
Spread miso on all sides of tofu slices, layering the slices.
Spread miso on sides and ensure that all areas are covered.
Place on glass plate and cover with bamboo mat. Let sit for
24 - 48 hours at room temperature.

Scrape the miso off the tofu and save for sandwich spread.
Keep the tofu cheese refrigerated until used.

I prefer using millet miso or chick pea miso. However, any kind
can be used. The stronger the miso, the stronger the tofu
cheese.

The tofu can be steamed for 5 minutes and then drained and
pressed.

Tofu Cheese Sandwich Spread

1 slice tofu cheese
miso from making tofu cheese
1 - 3 tsp tahini

Mash 1 slice tofu cheese.
Heat the miso in small skillet, add tahini and stir 1 minute. Add
mashed tofu cheese and stir 2 - 3 minutes until it is well mixed
and smooth. Remove from heat. Serve warm or cold. Keep
refrigerated until used.

Great served warm on bagels or flatbread.

Sauerkraut / Cheese Sandwich

Rinse 1 tbsp sauerkraut and heat.
Heat 2 tbsp tofu cheese sandwich spread.
Spread heated tofu cheese sandwich spread on toasted rye
bread and top with heated sauerkraut This can be served open
or closed.

Tofu Cutlets — Miso Sauce

1 lb firm tofu
2- 4 tbsp miso (barley, millet, rice or chickpea)
2 - 4 tbsp hot water
1-2 tsp tahini
1-2 tsp barley malt or rice malt
1/2-1 tsp umeboshi vinegar

Cut tofu in cutlets about 2"x 3" and 1/4" - 1/2" thick. Press for
1/2 hour to remove water.
Purée miso in hot water, add tahini, barley malt and umeboshi
vinegar.
Spread miso on cutlets and bake on lightly oiled cookie sheet for
15 - 20 minutes at 350° F.

Servings 4 - 6

Breaded Tofu Cutlets

1 lb firm tofu
2 tbsp tamari
2 tbsp water
1 tsp grated ginger

1/3 cup cornmeal
1/3 cup brown rice flour

Cut tofu in cutlets about 2" x 3" and 1/2" - 3/4" thick. Press for 1/2 hour to remove water. Combine tamari, water and grated ginger and marinate tofu for 15 minutes.
Combine cornmeal and flour and coat the tofu cutlets. Place on well-oiled cookie sheet, turn over before cooking so there is a bit of oil on the top, and bake at 350° F for 30 minutes, turning once during cooking. If there is not enough oil, the cornmeal will be dry and hard.
These will be tough on the outside and soft inside. For a firmer cutlet cut slices 1/2" thick instead of 3/4".
Serve with onion gravy.

Servings 4 - 6

One grain can yield ten thousand grains;
One idea can lead to a goal;
> *A grain is only one grain until it is planted.*
> *An idea is only an idea until it is acted upon.*
Take the first step and reap the abundant harvest.

Tofu Steak

A 1 lb firm tofu
   2 -3 tsp tamari
   2 tsp water
   1/2 tsp grated ginger
   2 tbsp sesame oil

B 3 tbsp diced onion
   3 tbsp grated carrot
   3 tbsp chopped mushrooms
   1 tbsp chopped scallions
   2 tbsp chopped parsley
   1 tsp tamari
   1/2 tsp mirin
   1/2 tsp umeboshi vinegar
   1 tsp sesame oil

Cut tofu in four slices (steaks) and press for about 1 hour to remove the water.

Prepare all vegetables. Sauté onion and mushroom in 1 tsp sesame oil for 3 minutes. Add the remaining ingredients in B and stir for 1 minute. Remove from heat and let sit covered for 5 minutes.

Heat 1-2 tbsp sesame oil in skillet on medium heat. Add the tofu steaks and cook for 5 minutes, gradually lowering heat to minimum, (if the pan is too hot when the steak is turned over it will burn). Turn steaks over and cook for 5 minutes, adding more oil if needed. Poke 10 - 15 holes half-way through the steaks with a chopstick. Combine 2 tsp water, 2-3 tsp tamari and grated ginger and pour over the steaks, filling the holes. Spread the vegetable mixture over the top of the steaks and cook for another 5 minutes.

Delicious served with noodles in gingery carrot sauce.

Variations
- Season to taste but watch the salt.
- For a sharper taste a few capers can be added to the vegetables.
- Capers, which are pickled flower buds of Mediterranean shrubs, can be found at most health food stores.

Chick Pea Patties

1/3 - 1/2 cup chick peas
1 medium parsnip
1 onion
1 tbsp tahini
1 tbsp tamari
1 - 2 tbsp sesame oil

Soak chick peas overnight or up to 3 days, changing the water daily.
Blend 1 cup soaked chick peas, tahini and tamari in food processor, to a coarse consistency.
Finely grate parsnip and chop onion. Add to the chick peas and mix well. Form into small patties which can be lightly coated with rice flour or kinako. Fry in lightly oiled skillet for about 5 minutes, turn over and cook covered for 15 - 20 minutes, being careful not to burn them. Or, fry for 5 minutes on each side and bake at 350° F for 20 minutes.
We are using raw chick peas, so it is important that they be well cooked.

Variations
- A small amount of water can be added when blending the chick peas. They can be dropped from a spoon instead of forming patties.

Said the robin to the sparrow:
"I should really like to know
why these anxious human beings
rush about and worry so."
Said the sparrow to the robin:
"Friend, I think that it must be
that they have no heavenly Father
such as cares for you and me."
Elizabeth Cheney

Lentil Burgers — for two

A 1/4 cup small brown lentils
1" piece kombu
1/4 small onion- chopped
1/4 small carrot-chopped
pinch of oregano
1/8 tsp thyme
3/4 + 1/4 c water
1 tsp tamari
1 1/2 tbsp medium bulgar

B 1/4 small onion - minced
1/4 small carrot - grated
3/8 cup large rolled oats
2 tsp tamari
1 tbsp chopped parsley

C 1 - 2 tbsp sesame oil

Break the kombu in very small pieces, rinse and place in small covered pot. Add the chopped onion and carrot, oregano and thyme. Pick through the lentils for stones, wash well and add to pot along with 3/4 cup cold water. Bring to a boil, cover, reduce heat and gently simmer for 45 minutes. Check lentils periodically and if dry on top, add 1/4 cup cold water but do not stir. Add bulgar and tamari and stir well to mix in the bulgar. Cook for another 15 minutes, stirring occasionally. Remove from heat and place in a bowl. Allow it to cool until it can be comfortably worked with the hands.

Mash lentils until 50% broken. Add 2 tsp tamari, minced onion, grated carrot and chopped parsley. Mix well.

Add the rolled oats and work with the hands until the mixture sticks together and can be formed in patties. With wet hands, form into patties — 4 small or 2 large. They will hold together better if allowed to cool completely before frying. Just before frying they can be rolled in flour or fine soygrits. Fry in small amount of sesame oil for 5 - 10 minutes on each side, depending on size of pattie.

Variations
- Warm cooked rice can be used instead of rolled oats.
- Can be baked instead of fried.
- Vary the amounts and kinds of herbs or seasonings.
- Served with onion gravy, it makes a delicious burger steak.

Shepherd's Pie

2 cups millet
1 small onion
1 cup cauliflower
5 cups water
pinch sea salt

1 tsp tamari
1 tsp water
2 tsp gomashio

2 carrots
1 cup water
pinch sea salt

1 cup seitan
2 tsp tamari
1-2 tsp arrowroot flour
1 tbsp cold water
1/2 cup green peas (frozen OK)

Press seitan for a half-hour and save the liquid.
Wash millet, chop onions and cauliflower and place in pot.
Add water and salt, bring to a boil, cover, reduce heat and gently simmer for 30 minutes. When cooked, mash but do not add more liquid.
Cut carrots in 1/2" pieces and gently simmer in 1 cup water and pinch salt for 5 minutes. Add peas, remove from heat.
Save cooking water.
Lightly oil a baking dish, line the bottom and sides with half the mashed millet. Bake at 350° F for 5 minutes.
To the remaining mashed millet, add 1/2 cup of the carrot cooking water and mash until smooth and creamy.
Slice, mince or cube the seitan.
Heat 1/2 cup liquid (liquid from seitan plus carrot cooking water) and 2 tsp tamari. Thicken with arrowroot flour dissolved in cold water. Add seitan, carrots and peas. Place in the baking dish and top with the remaining mashed millet. Mix 1 tsp tamari and 1 tsp water and drizzle over millet. Sprinkle with gomashio. Bake at 350° F for 10 - 20 minutes.

Servings 4 - 6

Variations
- Tempeh, tofu or beans can be used instead of seitan.
- Millet can be cooked with carrots or squash.

46

Paté Chinois — for two

1/4 onion
1 tsp sesame oil
1/2 cup seitan
1/4 cup liquid
1 tsp tamari
1 tsp arrowroot flour
2 tbsp cold water

1/2 cup corn
1/2 cup water
pinch sea salt

1/2 cup millet
1/4 onion
1/4 c cauliflower
1 1/2 cups water
pinch sea salt

1/2 tsp tamari
1/2 tsp water
1 tsp gomashio

Press seitan for one half hour and save the liquid.

Chop onion and cauliflower fine.
Wash millet well.
Place onion, cauliflower and millet in small pot with tight-fitting cover. Add salt and water. Bring to a boil, cover, reduce heat and gently simmer for 30 minutes.
When cooked, mash until smooth.

Simmer corn in 1/2 cup water and a pinch of salt for 10 minutes. Use the cooking water in the seitan. Remove corn from water, purée until half the kernels are broken.

Chop the onion fine and saute in 1 tsp sesame oil for 2 minutes. Mince the seitan and add to the onions. Add 1/4 cup liquid (liquid from the seitan plus corn cooking water). Add tamari and simmer for 5 minutes. Thicken with arrowroot flour dissolved in cold water.

In a lightly oiled baking dish layer: seitan, corn, mashed millet. Mix 1/2 tsp tamari and 1/2 tsp water and drizzle over millet. Sprinkle with 1 tsp gomashio. Bake at 350° F for 10 - 20 minutes.

Shiva said "Step out of the river of conditioning and see the world as if for the first time".

Tourtière

A 8 oz tempeh
1 cup water
1 tsp tamari
1 onion - chopped
1 carrot - grated
1 tbsp gomashio
2 -3 tsp tamari
1 tsp umeboshi vinegar
1 tsp mirin
1 tsp summer savory
1/2 cup water
1 tsp arrowroot flour
dissolved in 2 tbsp cold water

B 1 1/2 cups water
1 cup whole wheat couscous
pinch sea salt
slice fresh ginger
1 tbsp chopped parsley

C 2 cups whole wheat
pastry flour
1/3 cup corn oil
1/4+ cup cold water
1 tsp umeboshi vinegar

A. Parboil tempeh in 1 cup water and 1 tsp tamari for 20 minutes, turning several times. Crumble tempeh, add remaining ingredients in A, gently simmer 10 minutes adding more water if needed. Thicken with arrowroot flour and stir until cooked, 2 - 3 minutes.

B. Bring 1 1/2 cups water to boil, add pinch of salt, slice of ginger and 1 cup whole wheat couscous. Stir with fork, cover, remove from heat and let sit for 5 minutes. Remove the ginger, fluff the couscous with a fork, mix in the parsley and tempeh. Mixture should be moist.

C. Pie Crust

Put flour in mixing bowl and stir in oil using a pastry cutter or two forks. The consistency should be pebble-like. Add the umeboshi vinegar and the water a little at a time and form the dough into a ball. Roll out half the dough. Place in a lightly oiled pie plate and bake for 5 minutes at 350° F. Roll out remaining dough for top crust. It is sometimes easier to handle if rolled out on waxed paper. Dough can also be chilled for 15 - 30 minutes before rolling. Fill pie shell, cover with top crust and bake 25 - 35 minutes at 375° F.

Tourtière for two

A 1/3 cup seitan - minced
  1/4 - 1/2 onion - chopped
  1/8 cup cauliflower - chopped
  pinch thyme
  pinch summer savory
  1 tsp gomashio
  1 tsp tamari
  1/2 tsp umeboshi vinegar
  few drops mirin

B 1/8 c whole wheat
  couscous
  1/4 cup water
  pinch sea salt
  slice fresh ginger

C 1/2 c whole wheat
  pastry flour
  1/4 tsp sea salt
  2 tbsp corn oil
  1-3 tbsp cold water

B. To 1/4 cup water, add a pinch of salt and slice of ginger. Bring to boil. Add the couscous, stir with fork, cover, remove from heat and let sit five minutes. Remove the ginger. Add all the A ingredients.

C. *Pastry*
Put flour and salt in a mixing bowl and stir in the oil using a pastry cutter or two forks, until the consistency is pebble-like. Add the water, a little at a time. Using a fork, or your fingers, form the dough into a ball. Divide the dough in half and roll out two 6" circles. Spread the filling over half of each circle leaving 1/2 inch all around, fold over the other half and press the edges together with a fork dipped in cold water. A pastry maker can also be used.
Bake at 375° F for 25 - 35 minutes.

Variations
- Delicious served with onion gravy.
- Seitan, tempeh or tofu can be used.
- Quinoa or fluffy millet can be used instead of couscous.
  Allow for the extra 20 - 30 minutes cooking time.

Fish

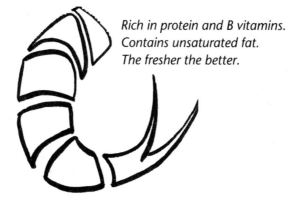

Rich in protein and B vitamins.
Contains unsaturated fat.
The fresher the better.

Avoid fish that is sprayed with chemicals.

White fish such as cod, haddock and halibut is OK for occasional use in moderation — 2 - 6 oz per serving depending on the individual's dietary needs. The following recipes are based on 2-4 oz per serving so they will be suitable for most people.

Shellfish
special occasions, when they are in season, and then in moderation.

In summer I like having a green salad with fish; in winter, cooked greens.

A small amount of grated, raw daikon sprinkled with tamari and served as a pickle will help to break down the fat in the fish, and aid in digestion.

Fish Cakes

2 cups millet
1 small onion
1/4 medium cauliflower
5 cups water
pinch sea salt

1 onion
1/2 lb fish
2 tsp tamari
1 tsp chopped parsley
flour
oil

Cut fish in 2" pieces and marinate in 1 tsp tamari and 1 tsp water for 1/2 - 1 hr.

Chop onion fine. Cut cauliflower into small pieces. Wash millet very well. Put onions, cauliflower and millet in pot, add salt and water and bring to boil. Reduce heat and gently simmer covered for 30 minutes. Mash.

Chop the onion in 1/2" pieces and sauté in just enough water to cover the bottom of the skillet plus 1 tsp tamari for about 5 minutes. Add fish and sauté for another 5 - 8 minutes.

Add fish and chopped parsley to the mashed millet and mix everything well together. When cool enough to handle, form into patties. Roll patties in flour just before frying. Fry in lightly oiled skillet about 10 minutes on each side. Cook them the way you like them, just lightly browned or crispy on the outside.

Variations
- The patties will hold together much better if they are cold.
- The patties can be made a few hours ahead and refrigerated.
- Grated carrots can also be used.
- The patties become soggy if rolled in flour too soon.
  Leftover fish cakes can be used the next day by heating in the oven.
- Leftover millet from one day can be used to make fish cakes the next day.

Freely you have received, freely give.
Matthew 10:8

Fish Loaf

A *1 1/2 cups millet*
1 small onion
1/4 medium cauliflower
3 3/4 cups water
pinch sea salt

B *1/2 cup whole wheat couscous*
3/4 cup water
pinch sea salt

C *1/2 lb fish*
1/2 onion
1 tbsp sesame oil
1 tsp tamari

D *1 small onion*
1 small carrot
1 tsp tamari

A. Chop onion and cauliflower quite small. Wash millet. Put onion, cauliflower and millet in pot. Add salt and water and bring to boil. Reduce heat, cover pot and gently simmer for 30 minutes. Mash.
B. Bring 3/4 cup water to boil. Add pinch of salt and couscous, stir with a fork, cover pot, remove from heat and let sit 5 minutes.
C. Cut onion in 1/2" pieces and sauté in sesame oil until brown. Cut fish in small pieces, add to onions and sauté 5 minutes. Add 1 tsp tamari and sauté for another 5 minutes.
D. Chop onion fine and grate carrot. Add to the mashed millet along with the couscous and the fish. Mix well and press into a lightly oiled loaf pan. Mix 1 tsp tamari and 1 tsp water and drizzle over the top.

Variations
- The fish can be sautéed with tamari, water and gomashio instead of oil.
- Leftover mashed millet can be used.
- Gomashio can also be sprinkled over the top before baking. Leftover fish loaf can be fried the next day.

Lord please bless our fishermen and keep them safe, and thank you for these wonderful gifts.

Fish Stew

2 small onions	1/2 lb. fish
2 medium carrots	1 tsp chopped parsley
1/4 medium cauliflower	1 tbsp sesame oil
12 yellow wax beans	pinch sea salt
12 green string beans	sprinkle caraway seeds (optional)
1 parsnip	1 - 2 tsp tamari
1 corn on the cob	sprinkle grated ginger
4 tbsp green peas	

1. Cut the fish in 1" squares. Marinate in 1 tsp tamari, 1 tsp water, chopped parsley and sprinkle of ginger for 1 hour, turning several times.
2. Boil the corn on the cob in 2 cups of water for 10 minutes. This cooking water will be used in the stew.
   Allow corn to cool and remove the kernels from the cob.
3. Cut the onion in 1/2" wedges and sauté in the sesame oil with a pinch of salt and caraway seeds until brown.
4. Cut the parsnips in 1/2" pieces and the beans and carrots in bite-size pieces. On top of the onions layer: parsnips, yellow beans, green beans, carrots and corn. Add enough corn cooking water to cover the parsnips and beans. Gently simmer for 15 minutes, adding more corn cooking water if needed.
5. Make a well in the vegetables and add the fish along with the marinating liquid. Place the peas on top of the fish. Break the cauliflower into flowerettes and place on top of the peas. Add more liquid depending on how you like stew. If a lot of liquid is preferred, it can be thickened in the last few minutes of cooking with a bit of arrowroot flour or kuzu. Simmer for about 8 minutes.
6. Season to taste with a bit more tamari if necessary. Gently mix everything and simmer for another 5 minutes.

Fish and Stuffing

8 oz haddock
1 tsp tamari
1 tsp grated ginger
1 tsp water

1 c whole wheat couscous
1 1/2 cup water
slice ginger
pinch sea salt

1 onion - chopped
1 carrot - grated
1/4 cup chopped almonds
1/4 cup chopped parsley
2 tsp tamari

Cut haddock in 3/4" pieces, marinate in 1 tsp tamari, 1 tsp water and 1 tsp ginger for 1/2 hour, turning several times.

Bring 1 1/2 cups water to boil. Add salt, ginger and couscous. Stir with a fork, cover, remove from heat and let sit for 5 minutes. Remove ginger before using.

Chop onion and grate carrot.
Fluff up couscous with fork. Mix in the onion, carrot, almonds, parsley, and tamari. Place half the mixture in a lightly oiled baking dish. Layer the fish on top and cover with the remaining couscous. Cover the dish and bake covered at 350° F for 15 - 25 minutes. Uncover and bake for another 5 minutes.

Variations
- Place the stuffing between two layers of fish. This will require more fish and less stuffing.
- Use cooked rice, quinoa or millet instead of couscous.

Seafood Casserole

8 small onions (about 1" diameter)
1 medium shitake mushroom
2 carrots
8 flowerettes cauliflower
8 flowerettes broccoli
16 snow peas
1/4 lb white fish

8 large shrimp
8 scallops
1 cup original soymilk
2-3 tsp tamari
1/2 tsp grated ginger
2 scallions

Soak shitake for 20 minutes in 1/2 cup warm water. Cut haddock in 1" pieces and marinate in 1 tsp tamari, 1 tsp water and 1/2 tsp grated ginger for about 30 minutes, turning several times. Cut shitake into small pieces. Do not use the stems. Cook in the soaking water for about 20 minutes, being careful to disgard the settlements at the bottom. Cut the carrots into diagonals 1/8" thick and add to the shitake. Cook five minutes.

In a rectangular pyrex baking dish, layer:
   - Marinated fish with the marinating liquid
   - Onions cut in half
   - Flowerettes of cauliflower and broccoli
   - Snow peas left whole
   - Carrots and shitake mushroom with the cooking water
   - Shrimp cut in half lengthwise
   - Scallops cut in halfs

Drizzle a tsp of tamari over all. Pour a cup of soymilk over these layers. Sprinkle with gomashio. If more liquid is desired use a small amount of hot water. Bake at 350° F about 20 minutes (about 10 minutes after the soymilk starts to bubble). Cut scallions on the diagonal and mix in just before serving. If desired thicken with arrowroot flour.

Lobster Stir Fry

1 onion	1 -2 tbsp sesame oil
4 mushrooms	1- 2 tbsp tamari
1 stalk celery	1/2 tsp umeboshi vinegar
2 medium carrots	1/2 tsp mirin
4 flowerettes cauliflower	1 tbsp gomashio
4 flowerettes broccoli	2 tbsp chopped parsley
8 snow peas	1/2 - 1 cup water
2 cups bean sprouts	2 - 3 tsp arrowroot flour
2 scallions	2 tbsp cold water
2 small cooked lobster tails	

Cut onion in thin wedges, mushrooms in slices, celery in thin diagonal slices, carrots in shavings, cauliflower and broccoli in small flowerettes, and scallions in thin diagonals. Leave snow peas whole. Cut lobster in small bite-size bits.

Heat oil in large skillet or wok to just under the smoking point. Add onions and mushrooms and sauté for 2 minutes. Add celery and sauté for another minute. Add carrots and cauliflower and sauté for 2 minutes. Add lobster, broccoli, snowpeas, and scallion roots and sauté for 2 minutes. Combine water, 1 tbsp tamari, umeboshi vinegar, mirin and gomashio. Add to the skillet and simmer for 2 -3 minutes.

Thicken with arrowroot flour dissolved in cold water. Add bean sprouts, sprinkle with 1 tbsp tamari and stir for 1 minute to coat and cook the sprouts. Add parsley and scallion tops and serve.

Variations
- A stir fry is a good way to serve foods that we have to eat "in moderation only", as a small amount goes a long way. Try shrimp, scallops,and organic chicken in this manner.
- Tempeh and tofu are great in a stir fry. Leftover breaded tofu cutlets (made firm) can be used.
- Season to suit your taste.
- Vary the vegetables.

Sea Vegetables

Rich in minerals. Calcium and iron, a concern for many, is found in sea vegetables.
They strengthen the intestines, digestive system, liver, and pancreas and help to purify the bloodstream.

Agar agar
a gelitan from seaweed. It is colourless, odorless and tasteless and is great in desserts. It contains calcium, phosphorus, iodine and trace minerals. Agar agar is sold in flakes, powder or bars, so read the directions on the package.

Arame
contains calcium, phosphorus, iron and potassium. Arame is shredded in long noddle-like strips and is delicious as a side dish or with rice, soups or stews.

Hijiki
an excellent source of calcium. Hijiki contains vitamins A, B1 and B2, phosphorus and iron, and is much like arame but stronger tasting and requires longer soaking.

Dulse
snacking food of Nova Scotia. It is rich in iron and contains potassium and magnesium. I use it in pea soup to replace the ham bone. Sautéed in sesame oil, it makes nice chips, and it is also great in salads or as a condiment.

Kelp
grows along the East Coast. It can be used in soup like kombu or wakame.

Kombu
used as a soup stock. When used in cooking beans, it makes them easier to digest. Kombu contains potassium, sodium and vitamins A and B.

Nori
contains calcium, potassium, manganese, magnesium, and phosphorus as well as vitamins A, C and niacin. Nori is toasted before using (much of the nori on the market has already been toasted). Use nori to make sushi. A sheet of nori, broken into 2" squares is delicious with any meal and helps to reduce the craving for fish. Used as a condiment or in soups, salads and stews.

Wakame
similar to kombu. It is used in soups, salads or stews. It contains calcium, niacin, iron, sodium and manganese.

Sea Vegetable Reference Books
Sea Green Primer by Juel Andersen
Cooking with Sea Vegetables by Peter and Montse Bradford

Arame

1/2 cup arame
1 small onion
water
1 - 2 tsp tamari

Rinse arame in cold water and soak in a small amount of water for 5 minutes.
Cut onion in thin slices.
Drain arame and cut in 1" diagonals.

Place onion in bottom of pot and add arame. Add enough water to just cover the onion (the arame is not covered with water). Bring to boil, cover, reduce heat and gently cook for 20 minutes, adding more water if necessary.
Add tamari and cook 5 to 10 minutes longer, allowing most of the liquid to cook off. Stir or shake pot just before serving.

Servings 4
Preparation time 10 minutes   Cooking time 30 minutes

I prefer not to use the soaking water as I find the taste too strong.
Arame is best when cooked in as little water as possible, cooking it in a lot of water makes it quite bitter. Stirring arame too soon will make the vegetables dark.

Variations
- Arame can be cooked with carrot or parsnip sticks, or using a combination of carrot and parsnips.
- Grated ginger can be added to the arame in the last few minutes of cooking.
- Arame and lotus seeds makes a delicious dish.
- A small amount of tahini can be added to the arame; I like this for festive meals.
- Roasted sunflower seeds can be added to the arame just before serving.

Hijiki with Sunflower Seeds

1/4 cup hijiki   2 tbsps roasted sunflower seeds
1 small onion   1 tsp grated fresh ginger root
2 tsp tamari   water

Rinse hijiki and soak 20 minutes. Cut onion in thin wedges.
Drain hijiki and cut in 1" diagonals. Place onion in pot. Place
hijiki on top of onions. Add just enough water to cover the
onions (hijiki is not covered with water). Bring to boil, reduce
heat and gently simmer for about 20 minutes covered, adding
more water if necessary. Add tamari and cook uncovered for 10
minutes, cooking off most of the liquid. Add grated ginger and
simmer for 2 minutes. Add roasted sunflower seeds just before
serving.

Servings 4
Preparation time 30 minutes   *Cooking time 30 minutes*

Hijiki and arame can be interchanged in recipes. However, the
soaking time for arame is 5 minutes and the soaking time for
hijiki is 20 minutes.

*In 1979 when I decided it was time to get out of the rut and on
with life, I attended a yoga weekend at the Kripalu Centre.*

*Yogi Amrit Desai, the founder of Kripalu, gave several talks
that weekend and passed on much hope and wisdom to the
participants. However, one statement that he made had a
profound effect on me. He said that if you want to improve
yourself do not start by making a lot of sacrifices that will be
impossible to keep. Instead, choose one thing that you like doing
that is good for you, pursue that and everything else will fall in
place in its own time.*

*On returning home I decided to learn to swim. That was the
beginning of my healing journey and I have never looked back.*

Vegetables

Vegetables are 25-30% of daily meals.
Three categories — root, ground and leafy.

Root/Stem — *Burdock, carrots, daikon, onion,
radish, parsnip and turnip.*
Ground — *cauliflower, broccoli, brussel sprouts,
cabbage, squash, pumpkin and string beans.*
Leafy — *Bok choy, carrot tops, chinese cabbage,
collard greens, dandelion greens, daikon greens,
kale, leeks, mustard greens, parsley, romaine
lettuce, scallion, turnip greens, and watercress.*

Variety in the vegetables and cooking
styles are important.
Vegetables are normally cooked but a small
amount can be eaten raw or pressed.

Cooking
steaming, boiling, baking, sautéeing or pressure cooking.

Cook vegetables which are in season and from your own locale
as much as possible. Choose light foods and light cooking for
the hot days of summer, heavier foods and longer cooking, like
stews, for the cold winter days.
Use local, organic grown foods when available. It is wonderful
when you can grow them yourself.

Vegetables contain many minerals and vitamins.

The question often is asked — why not potatoes?
Potatoes, along with tomatoes, red, green and chili peppers and
eggplant are members of the nightshade family. These plants
are tropical in origin, some have toxic properties, and the leaves
of some contain the poison solanin. Nightshades are high in
alkaloids. Akaloids have been referred to as denatured proteins.

61

Instead of being tissue-builders, they are stimulants, hallucinogens, medicines and poisons. Regular use of tomatoes, potatoes and eggplant is believed to cause arthritis. Nightshade foods also effect the calcium balance. On a diet that is high in meat and dairy the nightshades might be OK but on a meat-free, dairy-free diet, nightshades are best avoided.

Also avoid members of the goosefoot family — spinach, swiss chard, beets and rhubarb because they are high in oxalic acid which interferes with the absorbtion of calcium into the tissues and cells.

Cauliflower and Broccoli (umeboshi sauce)

1/4 cauliflower
1/4 broccoli
pinch sea salt
water

Sauce
1 umeboshi plum
1/2 tsp rice syrup
1/4 cup water

Put about 1" water in pot, add salt and bring to boil.

Break cauliflower into flowerettes, remove any damaged or brown spots, wash and drop in the boiling water. Cook 3 - 5 minutes or until tender. Remove and place in warm bowl.

Wash broccoli, cut into flowerettes. Peel stems if tough and cut in 1" diagonals, put in the boiling water and cook 3 minutes. Add flowerettes and cook for 2 minutes or until bright green and still crisp. Remove and add to the dish with the cauliflower.

Sauce
In a suribachi, a grinding bowl, purée the umeboshi plum, rice syrup and water to a smooth consistency.
Pour over the cauliflower and broccoli.

Servings 4
Preparation time 10 minutes   *Cooking time 12 minutes*

I prefer only cooking greens until they reach the peak of their brightness. Once they become dark they lose their eye appeal, some of their food value and some of their delicious taste.

The Bible teaches us not to judge.
We know this means not to judge our fellow man, brothers and sisters all, but we conveniently ignore the fact that it also means not to judge self.
Don't be so hard on yourself.

Steamed Carrots and Broccoli
using stackable bamboo steamers

4 medium carrots
small broccoli
water
pinch sea salt

Put about 1" of water in pot and bring to boil.
Wash carrots with vegetable brush, or peel if not organic. Slice
quite thin on the diagonal, place in bamboo steamer, sprinkle
with pinch of sea salt. Place steamer on pot of boiling water,
cover and steam 6 to 8 minutes.
Cut broccoli from stalk leaving about 2" of stem attached to the
flowerettes. Peel stems of broccoli, if tough, and slice about 1/4"
diagonals. Place the slices stems in second steamer and place on
top of carrot steamer and steam for about 2 to 3 minutes. Place
flowerettes on top and steam for another to to 3 minutes.
Do not over-steam broccoli, cook only until a bright green.

Servings 4
Preparation time 10 - 15 minutes   *Cooking time 15 minutes*

*One day I decided that I was ready to learn more and grow so I
began this earth life. I entered a cocoon which I called my body,
and my body, mind and soul started the cycle. In the baby years,
my growth was mainly body. As the growth of my body slowed,
the growth of my mind speeded up. Finally the body stopped
growing (just maintenance now), but the mind was at its peak of
learning and the soul's learning was starting. Now that I am in
the last half of my life, the learning of the mind is more keeping
up with things than new explorations, but the soul is longing for
more and more knowledge of the spirit, connection with the higher
self, Universal Law, whatever we prefer to call it.*

*When I have learned the lessons for this earth life I will leave
my cocoon, taking with me all the knowledge that I have gleaned,
and emerge transformed, like a beautiful butterfly.*

This wonderful journey, from birth to death, we call life.

Lotus Root with Ginger Miso Sauce

1/4 cup dried lotus root
water
1/2 - 1 tsp grated ginger
1 tsp light miso
parsley

Soak lotus root for 4 - 5 hours.
Slice very thin.
Simmer in small amount of water (just covered) for about
1 hour, adding more water if necessary.
Purée miso, add to lotus root and simmer 5 minutes
Garnish with parsley or add chopped parsley just before serving.

Servings 4
Soaking time 5 hours
Preparation time 5 minutes   *Cooking time 65 minutes*

Variations
- Fish may be cooked with this.
- Fresh lotus root does not require soaking.

YOUR CHOICE!

I can't	*I can, I will, I am*
I'll do this tomorrow	*I'll start right now*
It's easier for you because-	*If others can do it so can I*
I don't have the time	*I'll make the time*
I can't afford it	*I'll budget*
I don't know how	*I'll learn*
I might not be able to do it	*I'll do my best*
I give up	*I'll try again*
Things always go wrong	*Things work out for the best*
I'm a born loser	*I have faith*

Squash and Onion (water sautéed with tamari)

1 onion
1/4 med squash - buttercup or butternut
1 tsp tamari - to taste
1 tbsp gomashio
water

Slice onions in wedges.
Wash squash well with a vegetable brush and slice in wedges about 5/8" thick. If not using organic squash you might want to peel it.
In large skillet combine water (about 1/2" deep), tamari and gomashio. Bring to gentle boil and add onions. Sauté for about 5 minutes.
Add squash and simmer 10 minutes or until tender.

Servings 4
Preparation time 15 minutes   Cooking time 20 minutes

Variations
- Serve the liquid with the squash.
- Thicken the liquid with kuzu and serve as a sauce.

The fun of being on a teeter-totter is going up and down.
After the rain comes the rainbow.
We need the rain and the sunshine to make crops grow.
A coin has two sides. In life everything also has two parts: birth/death, joy/sorrow, ups/downs, love /fear.
Unfortunately, we judge — this is "good" or this is "bad". We strive to have only the "good" and will try to avoid the "bad" at all costs. The cost of going for the one-sided coin is very high, as it is impossible, and causes disharmony, disease and lack of balance. The opposites are a natural part of life. Accepting this and honoring them for what they are is an important step in finding balance, harmony and inner peace.

Baked Whole Squash

1 small organic buttercup squash

Wash with vegetable brush.
Place in oven and bake at 375° F for 30 - 60 minutes, until cooked. Test for tenderness with a toothpick or a cooking chopstick.

Servings 4 - 6
Preparation time 5 minutes   Cooking time 60 minutes

Baked Stuffed Squash

1 small organic buttercup squash
1/3 cup cranberries   1 tsp kuzu
1/8 cup walnuts   2 tbsp barley malt
1/8 cup raisins   water

Wash squash with vegetable brush. Cut top out of the squash and save the top for the cover. Scoop out all the seeds.
Cook the cranberries and raisins with a little water until the cranberries start to pop. Add the barley malt. Mix the kuzu with about 2 tbsps cold water and add to the cranberries. Stir until cooked. Mix the walnuts in and pour into the squash. Cover with the top of the squash and bake at 375° F for 30 - 60 minutes or until cooked.

Servings 4 - 6
Preparation time 15 minutes   Cooking time 60 minutes

This dish is great at Thanksgiving or Christmas.

There are many paths leading to the one truth.

Turnip and Squash

1 small turnip
1/2 small buttercup squash
pinch sea salt
water
drops of tamari
sprinkle of gomashio

Peel and cube turnip. Place in pot with about 5/8" water and
pinch of sea salt. Bring to boil, lower heat and gently cook for
10 minutes.
Peel and cube squash, add to turnip and cook for 10 minutes or
until vegetables are tender.
Drain off water and save for soup.
Mash, adding a few drops of tamari and a sprinkle of gomashio.

Servings 4
Preparation time 10 minutes   Cooking time 30 minutes

Each December I look forward to the new edition of "The
Friendship Book" by Francis Gay. This book makes wonderful
Christmas gifts and I also buy one for myself. As I read the book
I jot the messages down on 3 x 5 cards and use them
throughout the house as uplifting thoughts for the day.
The following is one of my favourites and it has been an
inspiration to many.

Doubt sees the obstacles,
*   Faith sees the way.*
Doubt sees the darkest night,
*   Faith sees the day.*
Doubt dreads to take a step,
*   Faith soars on high.*
Doubt whispers, "Who believes?"
*   Faith answers "I".*

The Friendship Book
Francis Gay 1990

Baked Cabbage and Carrots

1/2 small cabbage
2 medium carrots
2 - 3 tsp tamari
1 tbsp gomashio
1/2 cup boiling water

Shred cabbage, grate carrots and combine. Place in covered baking dish, sprinkle with gomashio. Add tamari to boiling water and pour over vegetables. Cover and bake at 350° F for 40 - 50 minutes until tender.

Serves 4 - 6
Preparation time 10 minutes   Cooking time 60 minutes

LIVE EACH DAY
    TO THE FULLEST

Yesterday's troubles are written in sand,
   Brushed out of existence
       by God's own hand ~
The things of the future
      our hearts may fear
Can all be resolved
     when tomorrow is here...
Out of a lifetime, these hours alone-
 The hours of TODAY
  are completely your own...
    So as each sun is setting
     there's reason to say,
"Thanks, Lord ,
   for your gifts-
    above all,
     for this day."
          Jean Kyler McManus

Stew with Fava Beans

1 tbsp sesame oil
1 onion
1 parsnip
1/4 turnip
2 carrots
1/4 buttercup squash (omit for Hallowe'en stew)
1/4 small cauliflower
2-3 tsp tamari

1 cup fava beans
3" piece kombu
2 cups water
1 tsp tamari

Soak fava beans overnight. Disgard soaking water.
Break kombu into very small pieces and place in pressure
cooker. Add soaked fava beans and 2 cups water. Cover
pressure cooker and bring to high pressure. Reduce heat to low
and gently cook for 1 hour. Allow pressure to come down
slowly. Add tamari and cook uncovered for 15 minutes.
(The beans will break up and make a wonderful thick, brown
sauce for the stew.)

Cut all vegetables in about 1" pieces.
Heat sesame oil in dutch oven and sauté onions for 3 minutes.
Add parsnip, turnip and carrots and sauté for 2 minutes. Add
fava beans and cooking liquid. Gently simmer for 20 minutes
adding more water if needed. Add cauliflower and squash and
cook for 15 minutes. Season to taste with tamari.

Servings 4 - 6
Preparation time 20 mins   Cooking time 1 1/2 hrs.

Variations
- Also delicious with aduki beans, lentils, or chick peas.
- Hallowe'en Stew on next page.

Hallowe'en Stew

Similar to Stew and Fava Beans on page 70 except the stew is cooked in a pumpkin.

Cut top off pumpkin and save. Clean out all the seeds.

Place pie plate upside down in stock pot. Add enough water to cover pie plate and add more during cooking if needed. Place pumpkin in pot.

Follow the recipe for Stew and Fava Beans to "Add fava beans and cooking liquid." Simmer for 5 minutes.

Place in pumpkin.

Add cauliflower, put top back on pumpkin and cover pot. Cook on very low heat for 2 - 3 hours. The slower it cooks the tastier it is. Serve by scooping out pieces of pumpkin.

Love and faithfulness will meet;
righteousness and peace will embrace.
Man's loyalty will reach up from the earth,
and God's righteousness will look down from heaven.
Psalm 85: 10-11

Nishime Vegetables

6" strip kombu	1/2 small turnip
1 onion	1/2 small squash
1 small parsnip	water
2 med carrots	1/2 - 1 tsp tamari

Soak kombu and cut into 1" squares.
Wash all vegetables and peel if not organic.
Cut carrots, turnips and squash into 2" pieces.
Cut parsnip into 1/2" pieces.
Cut onion into quarters or 6 wedges.

Layer kombu, onions, parsnips, turnips and carrots in pot.
Sprinkle a few drops of tamari over vegetables. Add about 1/2"
water to start and add more during cooking if necessary. Cover
and turn heat high until a good steam is generated. Lower heat
and cook gently 10 minutes. Add squash and cook for another
10 - 15 minutes. When the vegetables are soft add more tamari
to taste and simmer 5 minutes. Most of the liquid will be
absorbed. Turn heat off, shake the pot to mix the vegetables
and liquid and let sit covered for a few minutes.

Servings 4
Preparation time 15 minutes   *Cooking time 30 minutes*

Variations
- There are many combinations that can be used: wakame can
  be used instead of kombu.
- Lotus root, burdock, or shitake mushrooms are very nice in
  nishime vegetables.
- The liquid can be thickened with a bit of kuzu.
- Sometimes I slice all vegetables 1/8" thick and for me this is a
  very soothing and warming dish when I am feeling tired or
  low.

Nishime cooking is very strengthening and warming.

Nova Scotia Hodge Podge

1 cup water
1 shitake mushroom
sea salt
1 onion or (6 small onions - walnut size)
6 - 8 baby carrots
1 small white turnip (apple size)
4 yellow beans
4 green string beans
3 cups original soymilk
scallions or green onion tops, for garnish

Soak shitake in 1 cup of water for 1 hour. Discard stem and cut mushroom into 1/2" pieces. Put mushroom and soaking water in soup pot. (Drain off the soaking water carefully to avoid getting the sediments in the hodge podge). Add pinch of salt and simmer for 15 minutes.
Cut all vegetables in small bite-size pieces except garnish. Add onions, turnip, yellow and green beans and cook for 10 minutes. Add carrots and cook for 5 minutes. Add soymilk and heat but do not boil. Salt to taste. Garnish with finely sliced scallions or onion tops.

Serving 4
Preparation time 15 minutes   Cooking time 30 minutes

Variations
- This is usually made with tender, young vegetables straight from the garden but is delicious at any time.
- I like including fresh broad beans. However, they will turn the hodge podge grey.
- As the name suggests it is a mixture so use whatever vegetables are ready at the time.
- Some people make it thick, like chowder, while others prefer it milky.
- Kombu stock can be used instead of shitake.

Greens

Organic Greens — soak in cold salted water to remove any grubs.
Cook in unsalted water. A few grains of salt can be added at the end
of the cooking.
Cook greens only until they reach the peak of green. Overcooking
makes them dark and not as tasty.
Greens can be steamed or boiled.

   Fresh young greens are delicious steamed.
   Older leaves become tough. However, they also are delicious
   if dropped in boiling water. Tough stems can be cut on the
   diagonal or peeled. Very tough stems can be used in soup.
Some greens like brussel sprouts are best if cooked uncovered,
otherwise they can taste bitter.

Brussel sprouts
are also good cut in half lengthwise and sauteed in a bit of oil
and gomashio, them simmered in a small amount of water and
umeboshi paste.

Sea peas
grow wild along the seacoast. Great if picked in the spring
before the buds appear and lightly steamed.

Watercress
is also tasty if lightly steamed. In the spring the wild variety is quite nice.

Bok Choy
can be steamed but is wonderful in stir frys.

Chinese cabbage and nappa
are delicious served with umeboshi sauce.

Turnip tops
are tender when picked before the leaves are about four inches long. After that they become tough and bitter. Drop in boiling water until they reach the peak of green. Great served with fish.

Carrot tops
are also very delicious. Very young ones can be chopped up and a small amount added to salads. Bigger ones can be steamed and mixed in with other greens or added to soup.

Kale
will grow late in the fall, until the snow covers it.

Dandelion greens and mustard greens are also delicious.

Variety and freshness in greens are important. Therefore it is best to buy in small amounts.
Serving 3 or 4 kinds of steamed greens together makes a delicious and attractive dish. Toasted dulse can also be added to this.

Pickles

A small amount with each meal or at least each day with the main meal
> *- aids digestion.*
> *- strengthens the flora in the intestines.*
> *- stimulates the appetite.*

Pickles can be made with salt, tamari, miso or vinegar.

The following recipes are for quick pickles. However, it is important to include good quality long-term pickles in your diet. These can be purchased at health food stores and include takuan, daikon, sauerkraut, ginger, baby dills, etc. When buying pickles it is important to read the labels for the ingredients.

If pickles are too salty it is best to rinse before serving.

Carrot Tamari Pickles

1 medium carrot
2 tsp tamari
2 tsp water

Wash and brush carrot with vegetable brush (if not organic carrot you might prefer to peel it).
Cut in flowers.
Place in pickle press.
Add tamari and water and press 2 - 4 hours.

Servings 4
Preparation time 5 minutes   Pressing time 2 - 4 hours

GIVE AND RECEIVE

We are told that in life we have to give and take, but I feel this should be give and receive.

To give is a blessing.
To receive graciously is giving someone else the opportunity to experience the joy of giving.

The Dead Sea is dead because it receives water but does not give any out and therefore there is no flow.
If we only receive and do not give we also soon become stagnant.
Also if we only give and do not allow ourselves to receive we soon become drained.

For many of us giving is very easy but receiving is something we have to work at.
Is the left side of your body stiff and the right side flexible?
Do you give easily but receive with difficulty?
We receive with the left and give with the right - could there be a connection between this and the stiffness?

Friendship is the masterpiece of giving and receiving.

Daikon Pickles

2" piece large daikon
2 - 3 tsp tamari
2 - 3 tsp water

Wash daikon with vegetable brush or peel if not organic. Cut in sticks or thin slices. Place in pickle press, add tamari and water (equal parts) and press for 2 - 4 hours. Rinse in cold water just before serving if the taste is too salty.

Servings 4
Preparation time 5 minutes   Pressing time 2 - 4 hours

Several years ago I moved into a flat that had been empty for many years. Friends who owned the house renovated the downstairs apartment with special attention to the kitchen, adding a large picture window in addition to the three existing ones. The side, which was practically all windows, faced the back yard of an elderly lady. In the morning I would sit in my kitchen and enjoy the splendour of my neighbour's garden, an array of gorgeous colours.

My kitchen was quite often full of friends who also appreciated the beauty next door. One day I went over to tell my neighbour how much I was enjoying her garden. However, before I had a chance to tell her this, she told me how she was so comforted by the light from my kitchen windows which was shining out in the back yard , giving it a very warm and friendly feeling. For so many years it had been closed and just looked like a black hole.

I enjoy having my curtains and door open and my neighbour said that it was heartwarming for her to see my friends and hear their laughter. By not having barriers between the two homes we were able to exchange and enjoy light and beauty.

This also is very true of life. We all are a source of light and beauty, but too often we build walls around ourselves, shutting ourselves in and depriving many a lonely soul of our true essence - light and beauty. To let this light and beauty flow back and forth we need only to open our hearts a little.

Mixed Pickles

1/2 small onion
1 small carrot
1/2" piece of daikon
1 cauliflower flowerette
1 broccoli flowerette

1 tsp tamari
1/2 tsp umeboshi vinegar
1/2 tsp mirin
1 tsp water

Slice all vegetables in small slices.
Place in pickle press.
Mix seasoning and add to vegetables.
Press 2 - 4 hours.

Servings 4
Preparation time 10 minutes   *Pressing time 2 - 4 hours*

A wave is not only a crest, it is also a trough.
A mountain is not only a peak it is also a valley.
   Life also has its highs and lows,
   its ups and downs,
   its valleys and peaks.
   The valley is equally as beautiful as the peak.
   It all depends on our perspective.

Onion Tamari Pickles

1 small onion
2 tsp tamari
2 tsp water

Peel the onion and cut in very thin slices.
Mix tamari and water (equal parts).
Place onion in pickle press, add tamari and water, and press for
2 hours. Onions become strong if pressed for more than
2 hours.

Servings 4
Preparation time 5 minutes   *Pressing time 2 hours*

Pickles may be rinsed in cold water just before serving.
Onions may be dipped in boiling water before pickling. This
takes away the sharp taste.
Leftover onion pickles go very strong so best to make small
quantities at a time.

There are may rocks along the path of life,
on some we will stub our toes;
others will be stepping stones to greater things or
a solid foundation on which to build.

It all depends on how we proceed along the path —
do we walk with our head down and drag our feet, or
do we look ahead, see the obstacles and turn them
into opportunities?

Red Radish Pickles

4 - 6 radishes
1 tsp umeboshi vinegar

Wash and brush radishes with vegetable brush.
Slice in thin rounds.
Place in pickle press.
Add umeboshi vinegar and press 2 - 4 hours.

Servings 4
Preparation time 5 minutes   *Pressing time 2-4 hours*

There are many teachers along life's journey —
from the ones who help us to take the first steps,
to the ones who take us to the summit.

I feel that these first teachers are a true blessing —
their roles not quite as glorious as that of the later ones.
Their tasks are much harder because without their love, patience
and dedication there would be no trek to the summit.

I am grateful for all my teachers but
mainly so for the early ones, who
            carried me when I could not walk,
            led me when I didn't know the way,
            pushed me when I was afraid to go further, and
            loved me when I made mistakes.

Condiments/Gravy/Sauce

In addition to adding extra flavour to the meals, condiments also add nutrients, balance, and colour. They stimulate the appetite and some have medicinal value.

Condiments are used in very moderate amounts.

Many condiments contain salt and the quality of salt is extremely important.

Do not eat too much salt. Salt is needed by most people. However, less is better than more.

In the hot, humid weather of summer we might need a bit more salt than we do in the below zero days of winter.

This is the extra flavour in the meal that we can control ourselves. It is very easy to overdo it as the condiments are so tasty. Use with awareness and appreciation.

A stream with no stones has no song.

Gomashio

1 cup sesame seeds (organic, unhulled)
2 - 3 tsp sea salt

Pick through seeds to remove sticks, stones and other unwanted matter.
Wash seeds and drain for a few minutes to remove most of the water.
Heat a skillet, add the seeds and dry roast* over low heat, stirring constantly so the seeds will roast evenly.
Roast until the seeds begin to pop and can be crushed easily.
Raw sesame seeds taste bitter and burnt seeds also taste bitter, but just right they taste wonderfully nutty.
Taste continuously as you roast them to get them "just right".
Remove the seeds and place in a suribachi.
Put the salt in the skillet and dry roast for a minute to remove the moisture.
Add the salt to the seeds and grind until the seeds are 80% crushed.

Variations
- Use shiso leaves instead of sea salt. Dry roast the leaves and grind with the seeds.
- Dulse or wakame can also be used in this way.
- When you are used to making gomashio you may add the salt in the last minute of cooking, being careful not to burn the seeds.
- Reduce the amount of salt if you eat a lot of gomashio with each meal.

*Dry roasting means roasting without oil.

This day is God's gift to you,
To live it with awareness and love is your gift to yourself.

Dulse Condiment

1/2 cup dulse

Wipe with damp cloth to remove dust and excess salt.
Dry roast in oven or skillet.
When dulse is dark brown it can be crushed for a condiment or ground into a powder in the suribachi.

Ground dulse can be used in gomashio instead of salt.

Many times we shut people out of our lives — we are afraid to let friendship happen — because "they might leave me" or "they might die" or "they might move away" and then I will be hurt, sad or lonely.

After the death of a very special young person, who I had known for only a few months, I was feeling very sad and vowed never again to let anyone close — it was just too painful when they left. Then beautiful memories started to flood my mind and I remembered his wonderful sense of humour, joyful laughter and beautiful spiritual views.

I then realized that I was so much richer because this person had touched my life even though it was only for the short time when he was preparing to make the transition from this world to the world of spirit. If I had shut him out of my life I would have deprived myself of knowing a very special person and of these memories.

The words of that lovely song "The Rose" have a deeper meaning for me now — "The heart afraid of breaking that never learns to dance". The dance of life does have its share of sadness and sorrow, along with joy.

Friendship, regardless of how long or short it is, is one of its most precious gifts.

Roasted Sunflower Seeds

1 cup sunflower seeds

Wash sunflower seeds and drain in strainer to remove most of the water. Dry roast for about 10 minutes over low heat, stirring constantly so they roast evenly and do not burn.
Remove from skillet while still hot and place in pyrex or stainless bowl.

A large skillet is best for dry roasting.
A few drops of tamari can be sprinkled on after they have been roasted and removed from the skillet. Shake the bowl to coat evenly. Wrapped in toasted nori, makes a delicious snack.

Several years ago, during a cold February blizzard, I went to the florist and bought some yellow carnations. The florist asked, "Are you having a dinner party tonight?" "No," I answered, "I was just craving chocolate." "Oh," she jokingly said, "And do the carnations taste the same?"

I then explained that due to hypoglycemia and an allergy to caffeine, chocolate caused problems for me and that when I craved it, instead of just depriving myself, I would treat myself with something else. Quite often when we crave something, we are not really craving that particular thing but what it represents to us — a treat, nurturing, attention, etc.

Yellow carnations give me a lot of pleasure and peace and therefore they fill in for many things that I no longer choose to have. These "other" treats were very important to me in my early days of healing through the macrobiotic diet. Now that my health is greatly improved I can weigh the odds and make a decision about what I want. I still crave chocolate and I am still allergic to caffeine — if I eat chocolate I will not be able to sleep that night and it will take me two days to get back on track. Is this chocolate really worth two days of my life? Each time I do this I think of and thank Helen for a quote she wrote in the front of a book.

"I am more attached to my life than to food."

Gingery Carrot Sauce

4 carrots
2 cups water
pinch sea salt

1 tsp grated ginger

1 - 2 tbsp arrowroot flour
3 tbsp cold water

Slice carrots very thin and boil in two cups of water with a pinch of sea salt for 10 - 15 minutes. Purée the cooked carrots along with a small amount of the cooking water. Return to the cooking water, add the ginger. Dissolve the arrowroot flour in 3 tbsp cold water and add to the carrots stirring until cooked — about 3 minutes.

Noodles in Gingery Carrot Sauce

4 servings of sesame, rice spirals
6 cups water
pinch sea salt

Boil water, add salt and noodles and cook uncovered for 7 - 12 minutes, depending on type of noodles.
Drain noodles, add to Gingery Carrot Sauce and stir well to coat all noodles. Let sit on minimum heat (just enough to stay warm) for 10 minutes.

Onion Gravy

1 tbsp sesame oil
1/2 onion
1 tbsp gomashio
1 cup water, vegetable cooking water or stock
2 - 3 tsp tamari
1 -2 tbsps arrowroot flour
1/3 c cold water

Heat sesame oil in skillet on medium heat (do not let it get hot enough to smoke). Slice the onion in thin wedges and sauté in sesame oil for 5 minutes. Add gomashio, 1/2 cup liquid and tamari and gently simmer for 5 minutes. Add remaining 1/2 cup liquid, simmer 5 minutes. Dissolve the arrowroot flour in cold water, add to the skillet and stir until cooked, about 3 minutes. Remove from heat as soon as cooked.

Variations
- Whole wheat flour can be used instead of arrowroot flour.

Ginger Glaze

1 cup of vegetable cooking water
1 tsp grated ginger
1 tbsp kuzu
2 tbsp cold water

Add the ginger to the vegetable cooking water and place on medium heat. Dissolve the kuzu in cold water, add to the vegetable cooking water and stir until cooked (clear) 2 - 3 minutes.

Variations
- Toss the vegetables in the glaze and serve.
- Tasty with poached fish.
- Try a few drops of lemon juice instead of ginger.
- Chopped parsley can also be used.

Salads

Three types of salad:
*   -boiled.*
*   -pressed.*
*   -raw.*

Raw and pressed salad are best during the hot days of summer, boiled salad is OK at any time.

Pressed salads are easier to digest than raw salads.

Salads eaten with fish help to provide balance to the meal.

The type, amount and frequency of salads will depend on the health and dietary requirements of the individual.

Watch that the dressings used with salads are not too salty.

Boiled Salad

1/2 Chinese cabbage or nappa
1 onion
2 medium carrots
pinch sea salt

Cut cabbage and onions into thin slices. Cut carrots into curls using vegetable peeler.
Put approximately 1" of water in large pot and add pinch of sea salt and bring to boil.
Cook vegetables, one at a time, from mildest to strongest tasting.
Cook cabbage 1 - 2 minutes. Remove and place in large bowl.
Boil onions 2 - 4 minutes. Remove and place in bowl with cabbage.
Boil carrots 1 minute. Remove and place in bowl.

Umeboshi Plum Dressing
Purée 1 umeboshi plum with 1/2 cup of water used to cook the vegetables. Add some gomashio to the dressing , pour over the salad and mix well.

Servings 4
Preparation time 15 minutes   Cooking time 15 minutes

Any remaining cooking water may be used in soup.

Vary the cooking time to suit your own taste and condition.

The 1990's — a time many will remember — a painful time, a healing time , a beautiful time. Mother Earth is cleansing — part of the healing process. Many individuals are going through a spiritual cleansing — the time of truth and light. Though painful at times, there is the hope and promise of love, peace and joy. The macrobiotic lifestyle aids our own healing and cleansing and also supports the healing of Mother Earth.

Pressed Salad

1/2 small Chinese cabbage
1 stalk celery
2 or 3 red radishes

1 small mild tasting onion
1 tbsp sea salt (approximately)

Wash all vegetables gently and carefully.
Shred cabbage and place in bottom of pickle press.
Cut celery very thin on the diagonal.
Slice radishes in very thin slices.
Cut the onion in thin circles.
Layer all vegetables in the pickle press and sprinkle each layer with salt.
Apply pressure and let sit for 30 minutes to 1 hour.
Rinse with cold water before serving.

Servings 4
Preparation time 10 minutes   *Pressing time 60 minutes*

Variations and Notes
- Most vegetables may be pressed in this way.
- Instead of a pickle press, a bowl can be used. Place a plate on the salad inside of the bowl and weigh this down with a clean rock or bottle of water.
- The salt and pressure releases the water from the vegetables. When the water reaches the top of the pressure plate reduce the pressure, otherwise the vegetables will become fibrous.
- The amount of salt is important as the water will not be released from the vegetables if not enough salt is used.
- Adequate pressure is also a factor in the water being released.

Fresh vegetables are a wonderful gift from Mother Earth.
As we sit down to eat our meal, let's take a minute and give thanks and gratitude for the many ways that our Mother the Earth provides for and nurtures us.

Quick Dishes

Soupy Noodle Dish

1 3" piece of kombu
1 onion
1 carrot
1/2 - 1 cup lentils

4 cups water
1 small stalk broccoli
2 - 4 tbsps tamari
1/2 tsp grated ginger
4 servings noodles

Cut onion, carrot and broccoli into small bite-size pieces.
Pick through and wash lentils.
In pressure cooker, layer kombu, onions, carrots, and lentils.
Add water, cover pressure cooker and bring to high pressure.
Lower heat and cook at low pressure for 15 minutes.
Remove from heat and let pressure come down slowly.

Bring a pot of water to a boil. Add salt and the noodles and
cook until done, approximately 10 minutes.

Remove the cover from the pressure cooker, add the broccoli,
tamari and ginger and cook for 5 minutes uncovered. (If lentils
are not completely cooked, add the tamari. Cover and cook for
another 10 minutes, then uncover. Add the broccoli and ginger
and cook for 5 more minutes.)

Drain the noodles, place in soup bowls and add the soup.
Garnish with parsley.

Servings 4
Preparation time 5 minutes   Cooking time 30 minutes

Soaking lentils overnight makes them cook faster and easier to
digest.

Noodles with Vegetables, Lentils and Miso Broth

A 1 onion
1 small stalk broccoli
1 carrot
1 cup cooked lentils
1/2 cup cooked arame
2 - 4 tsp miso
1/4 tsp grated fresh ginger
3 - 4 cups water
parsley for garnish

B 4 servings noodles
pinch sea salt
slice ginger

C 1/2 umeboshi plum

A and B below can be cooking at the same time.

A. Cut onions, carrots and broccoli into 1/2" pieces.
Put water and onions in pot and bring to boil.
Lower heat, add carrots and simmer gently for 5 minutes
Add lentils and arame and simmer for 2 minutes.
Add broccoli and simmer for 2 minutes.
Purée miso, add to pot and simmer 2 minutes.

B. Bring a pot of water to a rolling boil. Add a pinch of salt if
the noodles do not have salt in them. Add a slice of fresh
ginger. Break noodles into quarters and add to the water.
Bring to boil and cook uncovered until done, 8 - 12 minutes
(noodle is the same colour all the way through when
cooked). When done, rinse with cold water to prevent the
noodles from sticking together. Remove the piece of ginger.

C. Make a paste by puréeing 1/2 umeboshi plum with wate
from the noodles. Mix this purée in the noodles.

Serve the noodles in a soup bowl with the vegetable broth and
garnish with parsley.

Servings 4
Preparation time 5 minutes   *Cooking time 15 - 20 minutes*

Variations- Tofu, tempeh or any other bean could be used.

Desserts

Don't throw out those favourite old recipes —
change the ingredients.

*Desserts contain sweeteners and the
quality and kind of sweetener is of utmost
importance. The sweeteners most
recommended in macrobiotics are rice
syrup and barley malt, both made from
grains. Sometimes combining the
two gives me the results that I
want.*

Raisins can also be used as a sweetener in cooking and baking.
Dates also, but not too much or too often.

Maple syrup is a very delicious natural sweetener. However, as it
is high in sucrose it should be used in moderation only. Some
types of commercial maple syrup may contain chemicals.

Many times we eat something and then feel quilty about it. The
feelings of guilt probably cause more problems for us than the
forbidden food does. If you are going to eat something then
enjoy it. If you are going to feel guilty about "cheating" then
don't eat it.

Tahini Apple Custard

3 - 4 large apples
1/4 cup raisins
1/4 cup roasted sunflower seeds or nuts
pinch sea salt
2 tbsp rice syrup
2 tbsp tahini
2 cups apple juice
2 cups water
2 - 4 tbsp agar (follow directions on package)
1 tbsp kuzu

Wash apples, cut into slices (if organic leave peel on unless tough or bruised).
In a saucepan, add water, juice, agar, apples and raisins and bring to a boil stirring to dissolve the agar.
When almost cooked add the rice syrup and tahini and cook until the apples are tender. Dissolve the kuzu in a small amount of cold water and add to the pan. Cook until clear, stirring constantly.
When cooked remove from the heat and allow to cool for 15 minutes and then add the sunflower seeds. Place in blender and blend until smooth.
Put in individual dessert dishes or a shallow baking dish and allow to set at room temperature before serving.

Servings 8 - 10
Preparation time 10 minutes   *Cooking time 30 minutes*

Variations
- Cinnamon may be added.
- Cranberries may be added.
- Cranberry nectar may be used instead of apple juice.

Dandelion Blend Jell

2 cups water
2 cups vanilla soymilk
3 - 4 tsp dandelion blend
2 tbsp rice syrup
agar (follow directions on package for 4 cups of liquid)
1 tbsp kuzu
pinch sea salt

Pour water into saucepan. Add agar and salt and bring to a low boil, stirring constantly. Lower heat and gently simmer until the agar is dissolved (about 20 minutes). Add the dandelion blend and rice syrup and stir for a few minutes. Add the soymilk and bring to a low boil, stirring constantly. Dissolve the kuzu in a small amount of cold water and add to pan and stir until cooked. It will be clear when cooked.

Put in blender and whip to make a nice foam on top.

Pour into individual serving dishes or a shallow dish.
Let cool at room temperature until jelled or put in the fridge to cool faster.

Servings 4 - 6
Preparation time 5 minutes   Cooking time 30 minutes

The dessert will be rubbery if too much agar is used.

Variations
- 1 cup of carob and 1 cup of vanilla soymilk may be used for a mocha type of jell.
- Rice Dream can be used instead of soymilk.

Quinoa Noodle Pudding

1 cup small flat quinoa noodles
   (or rotini)
pinch of sea salt
3 cups water
1 apple, cubed
1/4 cup raisins

1 tbsp rice syrup
1 tbsp tahini
cinnamon to taste (or ginger)
1 cup vanilla soymilk
1/4 cup roasted sunflower seeds

Bring the water to a boil, add a pinch of salt and the noodles.
Cook for 3 - 5 minutes. Drain noodles and rinse under cold
water. Using the same pot, combine the apples, raisins, rice
syrup, tahini, cinnamon and soymilk and bring to the boiling
point. Add the noodles and pour into a glass baking dish.
Spread roasted sunflower seeds over top.
Bake at 350° F for 10-20 minutes. The cooking time will
determine the consistency. Experiment and enjoy.

A FLEETING THOUGHT
            or is it?
Did that thought really just pass by
         or did you give it a permanent home?
Take "He's a pain in the neck."
*"Mind/Body" advocates might not just assume that the thought
actually passed by.*
*While we cannot change or control all the situations that we
encounter each day, we can change our way of thinking using the
"Own and Identify" technique.*
         -He's a pain in the neck
                  "I" don't like paying attention to small details.
         -She drives me crazy
                  "I" lose my focus
         -Keep a stiff upper lip
                  "I" don't want to show my feelings
         -Get off my back
                  *"I" procrastinate and don't like to be
                  reminded of it.*

Rice Cookies

1/2 cup sweet brown rice
1/2 cup brown rice
1 1/4 cup water
pinch sea salt

Wash and pressure cook as for regular rice.

When cooked, allow to cool for about 10 minutes then pound rice until grains are 50% crushed.

Add 1 - 2 tbsp rice syrup or barley malt.
Add 1/3 cup currants which have been reconstituted.

Mix well. When cool enough to handle, form into balls and roll in roasted sesame seeds, roasted and ground sunflower seeds — or roasted and ground nuts.

Bake at 350° F for 10 to 20 minutes.

Variations
- The seeds or nuts can also be mixed in with the rice along with the currants.
- Raisins can be used instead of currants.
- Rice malt and barley malt can be omitted.
- The rice can be cooked with juice.
- These can be made with all sweet brown rice or all brown rice instead of half and half. The brown rice is not as sticky as the sweet brown rice and will not hold together as well.

Sometimes when we are in disagreement with the lifestyle or actions of our fellowman, we tend to quote the bible to prove that this person is not living in accordance with the scriptures. How conveniently we forget that these same scriptures tell us "thou shall not judge".

Pumpkin Pie

A 1 medium hokkaido pumpkin
pinch of sea salt
1 tbsp agar agar
1 3/4 cup water

C pinch ground cloves
sprinkle of cardamon
sprinkle of cinnamon
sprinkle of pumpkin pie
spice
2 tbsp tahini
2 tbspbarley malt
1/4 cup raisins
2 - 4 tbsp arrowroot flour
1/4 - 1/2 cup cold water

B 1 cup whole wheat couscous
1/2 cup unsweetened granola
1 1/2 cups water or apple juice

D (optional)
10 chestnuts
2 cups water
1/4 - 1/2 cup soymilk

E (optional)
1/2 cup cranberries
1/4 cup water
1 tbsp barley malt
1 tsp arrowroot flour
2 tbsp cold water
2 tbsp ground almonds

A. Peel and cube the pumpkin. Put in sauce pan with water, salt and agar agar and cook until soft.

B. Bring 1 1/2 cups water to a boil, add couscous and stir with a fork. Cover pot, remove from heat and let sit for 5 minutes. Add granola and mix well. Press into lightly oiled pie plate and bake at 350° F for 5 minutes.

C. Purée the cooked pumpkin with any remaining cooking water and return to the saucepan. Add the spices, tahini, raisins and barley malt and bring to the boiling point. Mix the arrowroot flour with cold water. Add to the pumpkin and stir until cooked, about 5 - 8 minutes.

Pour the pumpkin in the pie crust and bake at 350° F for approximately 20 minutes.

D. Cut a cross in the end of each chestnut and cook for 20 minutes in 2 cups of gently boiling water. Drain, allow to cool and then peel. Purée, add soymilk and purée again until the consistency is thick and creamy. (It will be grainy, not smooth)

E. Cook the cranberries in a saucepan with water until they start to pop. Add barley malt. Disolve the arrowroot flour in cold water, add to the cranberries and stir until cooked. Remove from heat and let cool slightly.

Spoon the cranberries around the edge of the pie, just inside the crust and sprinkle with ground almonds.
Top off with a dollop of chestnut purée on each serving.

Variations
- Buttercup squash can be used instead of hokkaido pumpkin.
- Try adding carrots to the buttercup squash.
- Omit the above spices and use ginger instead. Adjust the spices to suit your own taste and dietary needs.
- Cook the pumpkin in a very small amount of water and add soymilk as you purée it
- Bake the squash whole and purée with a small amount of water or soymilk. This will require less agar agar and arrowroot flour. The consistency will be denser, rather than like custard. (It is easier if the seeds are removed before baking).

Crispy Squares

1/2 cup rice syrup
1/2 cup barley malt
pinch sea salt
1/2 cup raisins

1/2 cup sunflower seeds or nuts
  (dry roasted)
1 box brown rice crisps

Using a deep skillet or dutch oven heat the rice syrup and barley malt to just under the boiling point. Add pinch of sea salt. Stir in the raisins, sunflower seeds and rice crisps making sure they are coated with the syrup. Spread out in a baking dish to cool. Cut into squares.

Servings approximately 20 squares
Preparation time 10 minutes

Variations and Notes
- Sprinkle some ground nuts or seeds in the bottom of the baking dish and the squares will not stick.
- Using a spoon dipped in hot water will make it easier to spread.
- If the rice syrup and barley malt is brought to the boiling point the squares will be very hard and crunchy.
- For an extra special treat I like adding two tbsp tahini, 1/4 cup each of unsweetened carob chips and hazelnuts. The tahini is added to the rice syrup and barley malt.
- Try combining other crispy cereals with the brown rice crisps.

Experiment with these. Try all kinds of combinations. Make them soft and sticky all the way to hard and crunchy. They will be great any way you make them and kids of all ages just love them.

Apple Cranberry Crisp

Fruit
6 - 10 apples
1/2 - 1 cup cranberries
1 cup liquid (water or juice)
pinch sea salt
2 - 3 tbsp rice syrup
1 tbsp kuzu

Topping
1 - 1 1/2 cups rolled oats
1 - 1 1/2 cups granola
1/4 - 1/2 cup corn oil
1/4 cup barley malt
1/4 cup rice syrup

Wash apples. (It is not necessary to peel organic apples.)
Slice apples about 1/4 inch thick and place in baking dish.
Wash cranberries and place on top of apples.

Put water or juice in saucepan, add salt and bring to boiling
point. Dissolve kuzu in 2 tbsp cold water, add to hot liquid and
stir until cooked. Kuzu becomes clear when cooked.
Add rice syrup, remove from heat.

Pour hot liquid over the apples and cranberries.

Topping
Put rolled oats and granola in a mixing bowl. Add corn oil and
mix well. Add barley malt and rice syrup and mix well.
I prefer using two forks to stir the syrup into the mixture.
Spread the topping over the apples, patting into place.

Bake at 350° F until the apples are tender and the topping is crisp
—about 30 minutes to 1 hour.

Serve hot or cold.

Servings 15
Preparation time 30 minutes   Cooking time 1 hour

All amounts and times are approximate as the type of apples
used will determine the amounts of apples, liquid and
sweetener.

Enjoy, enjoy — this is a guilt-free dessert.

Apple Corncake

A *2 cups whole wheat pastry flour*
1 1/2 cups cornmeal
5 tsp baking powder

B *2 tbsp tahini, 6 tbsps water or soymilk*
4 tbsp corn oil
1 tbsp barley malt
2 tbsp rice syrup
2 cups soymilk
1/3 cup reconstituted raisins

C *3 apples*

Preheat oven to 350° F.
Lightly oil a rectangular pyrex dish.
Slice apples about 1/4 inch thick, layer in pyrex dish and put in preheated oven for 5 to 10 minutes to warm apples. Apples should be warm, not hot.

Mix wet ingredients, B. In a separate bowl, mix dry ingredients, A. When the apples are ready, combine wet and dry ingredients and pour over warm apples and bake at 350° F about 45 minutes, or until a toothpick comes out clean.

To reconstitute raisins, boil raisins in 1 cup of water for about 1 minute and drain.
If the apples are cold, the cornmeal next to the apples will not cook dry. If the apples are too hot, the cornmeal will cook before rising. If either should happen the dish is still delicious, it just is not the texture of corncake.

Poppy seeds make a nice addition.

Wait on the Lord: be of good courage, and he shall strengthen thine heart.   *Psalm 27:14*

Apple Gingerbread Dessert

3 apples
1 cup cranberry tea or juice
1 tsp kuzu in 1/4 cold water

Lightly oil a rectangular pyrex baking dish. Slice apples about 1/4 inch thick and place in bottom of baking dish.
Heat tea or juice in pot, mix kuzu in cold water, add to juice and stir until cooked. Pour juice over apples and place in oven at 350° F for 15 minutes.

Dry ingredients	Wet ingredients
3/4 cup whole wheat pastry flour	*1/2 to 3/4 cup vanilla soy milk*
1/4 cup corn flour or	*1 tbsp tahini +*
brown rice flour	*1 1/2 tbsp soy milk*
1/4 cup soya milk powder	*1/4 cup corn oil*
1 tsp baking powder	*1/2 cup barley malt*
sprinkle of pumpkin pie spice,	*1/2 tsp mellow miso*
all spice, cinnamon and cardamon.	*1 tbsp grated peeled ginger*
3 crushed cloves	

Blend wet ingredients. Mix dry ingredients in a separate bowl. Combine wet and dry ingredients and pour over warm apples (if apples are hot, allow to cool before adding the batter).
Bake at 350° F for 1/2 - 3/4 hour

Variations
- Eliminate the spices or adjust to suit your own taste and dietary needs.
  Raisins can be added to the apples.
- Sunflower seeds can be added to the dry ingredients.

You can be your own best friend or your worst enemy.
Fortunately, the choice is yours.

Baking Powder Biscuits

1 1/2 cups whole wheat pastry flour
1/2 cup corn flour
2 - 3 tsp baking powder - aluminum free
3 pinches salt
4 tbsp corn oil
2/3 cup cold original soymilk
sesame oil to oil cookie sheet

Sift together dry ingredients. Mix in oil with 2 forks or pastry cutter. Quickly mix in milk. Knead for several seconds on a lightly floured pastry board.
Pat out to about 1/2 inch thick and cut with cookie cutter.
Place about 1 inch apart on a lightly oiled cookie sheet and bake at 450° F for about 10 - 12 minutes. Baking time will depend on the size of the biscuits.

Variations
- Raisins can be added.
- For a sweet biscuit, vanilla soymilk can be used.
- A small amount of rice syrup, maple syrup or barley malt can be added.
- Use 1 cup of soymilk instead of 2/3 and drop biscuits from a spoon instead of patting out.
- For Onion Biscuits, add 1 grated onion.

*Do not go
        where the path
              may lead,
Go instead
        where there is no path
              and leave a trail.*
- Emerson

Cinnamon Pinwheels

2 dozen pinwheels		8 pinwheels
	Pastry	
2 cups	whole/wheat pastry flour	2/3 cup
1/4 tsp	sea salt	1/8 tsp
8 tbsp	corn oil	2 1/2 tbsp
4 tbsp	maple syrup	1 tbsp
2- 4 tbsp	cold water	1 - 3 tbsp
	Filling	
1/2 cup	currants - reconstituted	1/8 cup
1/2 cup	chopped walnuts	1/8 cup
1/2 cup	unsweetened coconut	1/8 cup
1 1/2 tsp	cinnamon	1/2 tsp
pinch	sea salt	pinch
1/2 cup	maple syrup	1/8 cup

In a mixing bowl combine flour and salt and stir in oil using a pastry cutter or two forks. Mix in the maple syrup. Add the water a bit at a time, using the fingers, and form the dough into a ball. Place dough between two layers of waxed paper and shape into a rectangle. Chill for 15 - 30 minutes.

Filling: Add the currants to 1 cup water, bring to a boil, simmer about 3 minutes and drain. Reconstituting currants or raisins makes them softer and sweeter and also reduces the oil or chemicals if they are not organic. Combine the currants with the nuts, coconut, cinnamon, salt and maple syrup and mix well.

Preheat oven to 400° F.
Roll out the dough between two layers of wax paper into a rectangular shape. Spread the filling over the dough leaving 1/2" space at top and bottom. Roll up firmly, using the wax paper as you would a sushi mat, and slice into 3/4" pieces. Bake on a lightly oiled cookie sheet for 10 - 20 minutes.

Ask not what your Country can do for you,
but what you can do for your Country.

Lemon Tarts

Pastry
1 cup whole wheat pastry flour
1/4 cup ground roasted almonds
1/4 tsp sea salt
4 tbsp corn oil
2 tbsp maple syrup
2 - 4 tbsp cold water

Filling
1/2 cup water
3/4 cup apple juice
pinch sea salt
1 1/2 tsp agar agar
2 - 3 tbsp arrowroot flour
1/2 cup cold water
4 1/2 tbsp rice syrup
2 1/2 tbsp lemon juice
grated rind 1 lemon
1/4 cup ground almonds

Combine flour, salt and almonds. Stir in oil until a pebble-like consistency using a pastry cutter or two forks. Mix in the maple syrup. Mix in the water a little at time and form the dough into a ball. Roll out, cut into circles and place in tart pan. Prick bottom and sides with fork.
Bake at 350° F for 10 - 15 minutes.

Combine water, apple juice, salt and agar agar. Bring to a boil, reduce heat and simmer for 15 minutes. Mix arrowroot flour in cold water. Add to the juice and stir until cooked (clear) about 3 minutes. Stir in the rice syrup, lemon juice and lemon rind. Cool for a few minutes.
Fill tart shells, sprinkle with ground almonds and allow to set.

Makes about 12 tarts.

We read and
forget some,
We hear and
remember some,
But, when we practice with awareness
We then understand.

Apple-Date Frogbellies

A   1/4 c dates (or raisins)
    1/8 cup water
    3/4 tsp umeboshi vinegar

B   2 apples
    1/4 cup water
    1/2 tsp lemon juice
    sprinkle of cinnamon

C   1/2 tsp kuzu
    1 tbsp cold water

Simmer dates, water and umeboshi vinegar for 5 minutes, then purée.
Chop apples fine (if organic, it's not necessary to peel them).
Add the B ingredients to the date purée and simmer 30 minutes on low heat, stirring often.
Thicken with kuzu dissolved in cold water and simmer for 5 minutes.

Makes 1 1/2 cups - enough for several batches of frogbellies.
Keep refrigerated.

Pastry

1 cup whole wheat pastry flour
1/8 tsp salt
3 tbsp corn oil

1 tbsp maple syrup
2 - 4 tbsp cold water

Combine flour and salt. Stir in oil until pebble-like consistency with pastry cutter. Mix in maple syrup. Add water a little at a time and mix to form the dough into a ball. Roll out between two layers of wax paper. Cut in 3" circles, put 1 tsp apple mixture on half the circle leaving 1/2" space all around.
Fold over and pinch the edges together (or use a pastry maker).
Bake at 350° F for 15 - 25 minutes.

Servings approximately 1 dozen Frogbellies

Variations
- Use mince(less) meat instead of apples.
- Vary the amounts of apples to dates.
- If you find dates too sweet, add a bit of umeboshi vinegar.

Christmas Pudding

A 1 cup whole wheat pastry flour
1 tsp cinnamon
1 tsp allspice
1/2 tsp ground cloves
1/8 tsp ground ginger

B 3/4 cup currants
3/4 cup Thompson raisins
1/2 cup sultana raisins
1/2 cup cranberries
1/2 cup chopped dried appricots
1/4 cup chopped dates
1/4 cup chopped prunes
3/4 cup chopped walnuts
1/3 cup bread crumbs

C 1 apple - grated
1 carrot - grated
rind 1/2 lemon-grated

D 1/2 cup corn oil
1/2 cup barley malt
1/2 cup ale
juice 1/2 lemon
1/2 tsp umeboshi
vinegar

Combine the flour and spices in A. Add the fruit from B, mixing each one in as it is added. Add the ingredients in C and mix. Combine the liquids in D and add in, mixing well.

Let sit overnight. Lightly oil one or two stainless steel bowls. Place pudding in bowls and cover with two layers of wax paper and several layers of aluminum foil. Make sure that the foil is tight so water cannot get in. To steam, use a tall pot and place a stainless steel pie plate upside down in the bottom of the pot to prevent the bottom of the pudding from burning. Stack the bowls. A second pie plate can be used in between the two bowls to make them more secure. Keep about 1 inch of water in the pot. Steam for about 8 hours.

Let cool. Remove wax paper and foil. When pudding is cold cover with dry wax paper and foil. Refrigerate until used. Steam about 1/2 to 1 hour just before serving.

Serve with your favourite sauce or try the "Lemon Sauce".

Lemon Sauce

1/2 cup water.
1/2 cup apple juice
pinch sea salt
4 tbsp rice syrup

2 tbsp lemon juice
grated rind of 1 lemon
2 - 3 tbsps arrowroot flour
1/2 cup cold water

Bring water and apple juice to boil, reduce heat to medium.
Add in salt, lemon juice, lemon rind and rice syrup.
Dissolve the arrowroot flour in 1/2 cup cold water. Add to the
juice, stirring until cooked, about 3 - 5 minutes. Remove from
heat, and serve warm.

Glaze
1/2 cup water
1/2 tbsp kuzu

Dissolve the kuzu in cold water. Cook on medium to high heat
stirring constantly until cooked (clear) 2 - 3 minutes.

Variations
- This glaze is clear and has no flavour. It can be used to glaze
  berry pies or fruit.
- A small amount can also be brushed on cakes or pie crust near
  the end of the baking time.
- To ice a cake pour the glaze over the cooled cake and sprinkle
  with crushed nuts.
- Apple juice instead of water makes a light golden glaze.
- For a yellow to orange glaze use orange juice and water.
- Cranberry tea makes a nice red glaze.
- The glaze can be flavoured with almond, lemon juice, vanilla,
  etc.
- Arrowroot flour can normally be used instead of kuzu.

1 tbsp of kuzu = 3 tbsp arrowroot flour, approximately..

Fruit Cake

A 1/4 cup Thompson raisins
1/2 cup sultana raisins
1/2 cup currants
1/4 cup chopped dates
1/4 cup chopped prunes
1/2cup chopped dried apricots
1/4 cup mixed peel (optional)
1/4 cup red cherries (optional)
1/4 cup green cherries (optional)
1/4 cup cranberries
1 clementine - chopped
1 small apple- coarsely grated
Peel 1/2 lemon - grated
Peel 1/2 orange - grated
1/2 cup chopped mixed nuts
1/2 cup roasted sunflower seeds
1 tbsp finely chopped candied ginger
   (optional)
1 tsp cinnamon
1/4 - 1/2 tsp ground gloves

B 2 cups apple juice
1 cup kukicha tea
3/4 tsp umeboshi vinegr
1 tbsp barley malt
1 tbsp maple syrup
1/3 cup corn oil

C 1 c apple juice
1 tbsp tahini
2 cups whole wheat
pastry flour

D Glaze
1/2 cup apple juice
1/2 tbsp kuzu
1/4 cup crushed nuts

Mix all A ingredients together.

Mix all B (liquid) ingredients together.

Combine A and B, mix well. Bring to a boil, reduce heat and simmer for 5 minutes stirring several times. Let sit overnight at cool room temperature.

Mix tahini in 1 cup apple juice and add to the mixture. Add the flour and mix well. Pour into a lightly oiled, floured cake pan (can also be divided in two). Bake at 350° F in preheated oven, for 1 1/2 hrs. When cool, glaze and sprinkle with crushed nuts.

To make glaze

Dissolve kuzu in cold apple juice, cook over medium heat, stirring constantly until cooked (clear). Allow to cool slightly and pour over cake.

Several ingredients in the fruit cake are marked optional as they contain sugar. These ingredients can be replaced with other fruits or the existing fruits increased by equal amounts. I find that by including the mixed peel and cherries I can serve this cake to people who prefer the Standard American Diet.

Mince(less)meat

A 6 small apples - peel,core and cube
1/4 cup currants
1/4 cup Thompson raisins
1/4 cup sultana raisins
1/2 tbsp grated lemon rind
1/2 tbsp lemon juice
3/4 tsp ume vinegar or 1/4 tsp sea salt
1 1/2 tsp oil
1 cup apple juice
sprinkle ground ginger
1/8 - 1/4 tsp allspice
1/8 - 1/4 tsp ground cloves
1/4 - 1/2 tsp cinnamon

B 1/4 cup water
2 tsp arrowroot flour
1 tsp miso

Combine all A ingredients. Bring to a boil, reduce heat to low, cover and simmer for 1 1/2 hrs stirring occasionally.
Uncover and simmer for another 1/2 hour.

Mix miso in 1/8 cup water and blend until smooth. Add to the apples.
Mix arrowroot flour in 1/8 cup water, add to the apples and stir until cooked about 3 minutes.
Allow to cool and then refrigerate until used.

Makes 1 3/4 cups

This will keep for several months in the fridge.
Great in tarts or frogbellies

Love is patient and kind.
Love never gives up;
and its faith, hope, and patience never fail
1 Corinthians 13: 4, 7

Breakfast Cereals

Porridge

Start your day right — have a good breakfast. You wouldn't expect your car to take you to work when it's on empty. Treat your body with the same respect and awareness.

Whole grains, "the staff of life", give us the steady, long-lasting energy we need to perform our work and play. They contain proteins, carbohydrates, vitamins, minerals and fat. Chew well as the digestive process starts with an enzyme in the saliva.

Brown rice
is the easiest grain to digest.

Soft rice
with a little umeboshi plum, is a good pick-me-up.

Sweet brown rice
when combined with other rice will make the porridge sweeter and creamier.

Feeling uptight and anxious? Try creamy barley porridge.

Millet
is a very warming grain. It helps to settle an acidic stomach and is good for the spleen and pancreas. It is a major grain for people with blood glucose disorders.

Oats
is also a warming grain and is high in protein and fat. The fat can cause mucous and therefore oats should not be eaten every day.

Quinoa
is high in protein.

Sweet Rice and Brown Rice Porridge

1/4 cup brown rice
1/4 cup sweet brown rice
1/4 - 1/2 tsp miso
2 - 3 cups water

Wash and dry roast sweet rice about 5 minutes.
Wash brown rice.
Put both sweet rice and brown rice in pressure cooker and add
water and miso. Cover pressure cooker and bring to high
pressure. Reduce heat to low and cook for 55 minutes. Allow the
pressure to come down slowly.

Servings 4
Preparation time 10 minutes   *Cooking time 60 minutes*

Variations
- Rice may be soaked overnight.
- Miso may be added after the rice is cooked. Purée miso with
  small amount of boiling water.Add to the cooked rice, cover
  pressure cooker and let sit 20 minutes before serving.

Autumn is a beautiful time of the year, a relaxing time.
The trees are wearing their finery of reds, yellow, magenta,
purple and gold. The rush and heat of the summer is over and the
cold of winter not yet ready to set in.
The autumn of life can also be a very interesting and relaxing
time. A slower pace, more time to do the things we want to do.
The heat is off and the cold has not yet set in. We also have our
own special finery, the knowledge and wisdom that life has given
us, and this we can now wear with comfort, no longer feeling the
need to prove ourselves. Autumn is the time to just be me.

Soft Rice and Quinoa

1/4 cup quinoa
2 cups cooked rice
2 cups water

Wash quinoa. Place in pot with water and cooked rice, bring to boil. Lower heat and gently cook for 30 minutes.
(Add more water for softer porridge)

Servings 4
Preparation time 5 minutes   Cooking time 30 minutes

Breakfast — Breaking the fast.

An important part of the healing process is rest and this includes the digestive system. The evening meal should be eaten at least three hours before bedtime so that the digestive system can also rest during the period of sleeping. This makes for a more restful sleep, because when we are sleeping our breathing is quite shallow. But in order to digest our food we need to breathe more deeply.

Therefore, if we eat a meal and go to sleep we create a conflict in our breathing pattern, one part is saying breathe shallow (I need to sleep) and the other part is saying breathe deeply (I need to digest this food). In macrobiotics we break the fast gently, with a light miso soup and cereal.

The rest of the meals should also be spaced so the digestive system is not working hard all day. It is good to feel a bit hungry before our meals. Unfortunately many of us have developed the habit of eating everytime we are hungry. When we break this habit and eat only regular meals with the occasional small snack, we find that our energy is much higher and calmer.

Barley Porridge (overnight method)

1/3 cup barley
3 cups water
pinch sea salt

Wash and dry roast barley.
Boil water with pinch of sea salt.
Add barley to boiling water and boil 10 - 15 minutes.
Place in thermos and let sit overnight.
In morning place in pressure cooker with more water if
necessary and bring to high pressure. Cook at low pressure for
20 - 30 minutes.
Let pressure come down slowly.

Servings 4
Preparation time 15 minutes   Cooking time 1 hour

Variations
- For a creamier porridge ,do not dry roast the barley.
- Follow the above recipe, but cook an additional 30 minutes
  uncovered adding more cold water as needed and stirring
  quite often. This makes a thick, creamy porridge.

This porridge has a wonderful calming effect. Great for anyone
with hypoglycemia.

*Today as I look out the window at the beautiful snow-covered
field I again marvel at the wonders of Mother Nature.*
   *Each snowflake is tiny but has its own unique and individual
pattern. One snowflake, alone, does not make much difference but
together, the snowflakes, in a very short time, transform the land.
Maybe we are like a snowflake — tiny, individual and sometimes
our efforts seem too small to matter, but when we combine our
efforts with the efforts of others, together we can make a
difference.*

116

Millet - Rolled Oats Porridge

2 - 3 cups water
1/4 cup rolled oats
1/4 cup millet
pinch sea salt

Wash millet well and dry roast, 5 - 10 minutes, until it releases a nutty aroma.
Add millet, rolled oats and salt to water and bring to a boil.
Reduce heat and cook for about 30 minutes.
Let sit 5 - 10 minutes before serving.

Servings 4
Preparation time 15 minutes   Cooking time 40 minutes

Got the blues, feeling low? Don't know what to do to change the feeling? There are many things that help.
- Go for a long, slow walk.
- Wash the kitchen floor, paying special attention to the corners.
- Read an uplifting book. There are great spiritual books available these days.
- Go swimming.
- Do volunteer work; a hugger in a children's hospital is great for the blues and is also very rewarding.
- Phone a friend and talk about something of interest to both of you — fashion, sports, hobbies, children.
- Go to a movie with a friend.
- Cook a delicious meal for a friend or two.
- Give yourself permission to sit for fifteen minutes and really feel the blues. Where are the blues now?
- Put some pretty flowers in your home.
- Get some small plants and give them tender, loving care and watch them grow.
- Smile!

Millet and Squash Porridge

1 cup millet
1/2 cup squash
5 - 6 cups water
pinch sea salt

Wash millet and dry roast for 5 - 10 minutes. Add salt to the water and bring to a boil. Carefully add millet to the boiling water. Add squash and bring to a boil again. Cover pot and cook over low heat for 30 minutes.
Stir well to blend in the squash.

Servings 4
Preparation time 15 minutes   Cooking time 35 minutes

Variations
- Millet can be cooked without dry roasting.
- Millet can be cooked without the squash. Cook squash separately and serve as a sauce over the cooked millet.

I read this wonderful quote —
     "God comforts the disturbed
          and disturbs
          the comfortable."
I have always known that God comforts in time of trouble, but it is reassuring to know that when I'm being SURE of myself —
(that's the times when I can do the most damage by being cocky, arrogant or ignorant) — that there's a Higher Power that loves me enough to say "Hey you, smarten up," and send me a little disturbance to help keep me on track.

Oat Groats Porridge

1/2 cup oat groats
pinch sea salt
2 1/2 - 3 cups water

Wash the oat groats. Bring water and salt to a boil, add the oat groats and boil for 5 - 10 minutes.
Put in thermos and let sit overnight.
In the morning cook over low - medium heat for 15 - 30 minutes, adding more water for the desired consistency.

Servings 4
Cooking time 45 minutes

Variations
- Dry roast for a nutty taste. However, the cereal will not be as creamy.

Oat groat porridge is a wonderful warming cereal on cold winter mornings — a great way to start a day of cross-country skiing.

Many times we complain about the cold and dampness of our winter weather. Adverse conditions we call it.

One bitterly cold day last winter, as I was moaning and groaning about the weather, I walked into my office and was treated to the most spectular frost patterns on the window that I have ever seen. There were twelve panes of glass in the window and each pane had its own unique pattern. Forgetting about the cold, I reached for my camera and shot about twenty pictures, marvelling at the beauty of each. I have enjoyed these pictures over the past months and given many copies to friends and artists. Without the so-called "adverse conditions" there would be no beautiful frost patterns on the windowpane.

There are many "adverse" things in life that also have a beautiful side but too often we are so wrapped up in our moaning and groaning that we don't see the beauty surrounding us.

Rolled Oats Porridge

1/2 cup rolled oats
3 cups water
pinch sea salt

Put cold water in saucepan, add salt and rolled oats and bring to boil. Lower heat and gently simmer for 20 - 30 minutes. Turn heat off, cover pot and let sit for 10 minutes before serving.

Servings 4
Cooking time 35 minutes

Variations
- Dry roast rolled oats for a nutty taste.
- Bring water to a boil and then add the rolled oats.
- Add the rolled oats to cold water and cook over very low heat. This takes longer, however, the result is a delicious, creamy cereal.
- Use less water for a thicker consistency and more water for a lighter cereal.
- Start with 2 cups of water, add more cold water as needed.
- My favourite is Sunday porridge —add raisins, roasted sunflower seeds, flax seeds, dash of cinnamon, and a tbsp rice syrup.

Meal Plans

Meal Planning and Cooking

One way to be sure that everything will be ready on time and nothing is forgotten, is to have a menu plan showing the ingredients and cooking time. A further aid is short or detailed cooking steps. This also is very helpful when several people are preparing the meal together or where there is a lot of activity.

A. *Menu*
Start with a simple format on a large sheet of paper. The format I use is on page 123.

B. *Planning*
This is done in five stages:
1) Plan the meal.
2) List the ingredients.
3) Calculate the preparation and cooking times.
4) On the menu shopping list, underline the things you need and take it with you when you go shopping. This makes it easier to get substitutes if you can't find exactly what you need.
5) List the cooking steps. This can be done at the bottom of the menu and continue on the back if necessary. If I'm trying something new I put down all the details I need so I can work just from the steps.

• When making a menu format include all the categories that you need.

• *Planning the meal:*
- allow ample time for cooking — cooking is almost as enjoyable as eating;
- colour is important;
- keep the meal fairly simple, unless it is a special occasion;
- pickles and condiments can be made ahead of time;

- dessert, if any, can be made ahead of time. Now that dessert is no longer a regular part of my meals, when I do have it I enjoy it a lot more.

- *Listing the cooking steps*
  - does anything need overnight soaking?
  - look at the cooking times and start with the longest;
  - consider stove space — rice can sit in the pressure cooker for quite awhile after it is cooked and therefore free up the burner for things that have to be cooked at the last minute like greens.
  - if several dishes have two or three steps, list all the steps for each dish and then put them in cooking order.
  - put down as much information as you need to make cooking easy. For some dishes I need only one word guidelines. For other dishes I need more detailed instructions. Refer to the Short Steps on pages 125 - 139. On the following menus and Short Steps, vegetables are shown as vegs.

The steps are simply guidelines and will differ with each cook. Make a note of any changes as you go and this will make it easier for next time. Vegetables also have a way of determining the cooking times. Remember Murphy's Law — if you have lots of time it will cook fast but if you are pressed for time it seems to take forever.

MENU

	Prep Minutes	Cooking Minutes

Soup

Grain

Beans/Bean Products/Fish

Sea Veg

Vegetables

Greens

Pickles

Condiments

Beverage

Dessert

MENU

	Prep Minutes	Cooking Minutes
Soup		
Watercress Miso	5	20
(kombu, onions, watercress, miso)		
Grain		
Mashed Millet	10	40
(onions, cauliflower, millet, salt)		
Beans/Bean Products/Fish		(soak 8 hrs)
Aduki Beans	10	1 hr
(kombu, onions, aduki beans, squash, tamari)		
Sea Veg		
Arame	10	30
(onions, carrots, arame, tamari)		
Vegetables		
Squash & Onions - Water Sauted	10	20
(onions, squash, gomashio, tamari)		
Greens		
Kale	10	5
Pickles		
Daikon - Tamari	5	2 hrs
Condiments		
Gomashio with Shiso Leaves	(prepare ahead)	
Beverage		
Dandelion Blend Coffee		5
Dessert		

Leftover aduki beans, arame and squash make a delicious soup the following day.

Mashed Millet / Aduki Beans
SHORT STEPS

1. Aduki Beans - soak aduki beans a minimum of 3 hours
2. Pickles
3. Aduki beans
4. Millet
5. Arame
6. Soup - kombu
7. Vegs - cut onions and squash
8. Kale - prepare
9. Arame - tamari
10. Soup - remove kombu, add onions
11. Aduki beans - tamari
12. Vegs - cook
13. Kale - water to boil
14. Soup - prepare watercress
15. Soup - miso and watercress
16. Kale - cook stems
17. Millet - mash
18. Kale - cook leaves
19. Dandelion Blend coffee

MENU

	Prep Minutes	Cooking Minutes
Soup		
Light Miso Soup	15	30
(kombu, onion, daikon, carrots, miso, parsley)		
Grain		
Short grain Brown Rice - Pressure Cooked	5	60
(rice, salt)		
Beans/Bean Products/Fish		
Lentils	10	60
(kombu, onions, carrots, lentils, tamari)		
Sea Veg		
(in soup)		
Vegetables		
Steamed Carrots	10	10
(carrots, salt)		
Greens		
Steamed Broccoli	5	5
Pickles		
Onion - Tamari	5	2 hrs
Condiments		
Gomashio	(prepare ahead)	
Beverage		
Kukicha Tea		10
Dessert		

Brown Rice Pressure Cooked / Lentils
SHORT STEPS

1. Pickles
2. Rice
3. Lentils
4. Soup - kombu, onions, daikon
5. Vegs - prepare carrots
6. Vegs - prepare broccoli
7. Soup - prepare carrots
8. Lentils - tamari
9. Soup - carrots
10. Veg - steam carrots
11. Soup - miso
12. Soup - prepare parsley
13. Tea
14. Veg - Steam broccoli

The Kitchen Prayer

Bless my little kitchen Lord.
I love its every nook,
And bless me as I do my work,
Wash pots and pans and cook.

May the meals that I prepare
Be seasoned from above.
With Thy blessing and thy grace,.
But most of all, Thy Love.

MENU

	Prep Minutes	Cooking Minutes
Soup		
Ginger Tamari Broth	10	10
(kombu, onions, carrots, tamari, ginger, scallions)		
Grain		
Brown Rice - Boiled	5	65
(rice, salt)		
Beans/Bean Products/Fish	(soak overnight)	
Chick Peas	10	90
Sea Veg		
(in soup)		
Vegetables		
Nishime	15	30
(kombu, onions, carrots, parsnips, turnips, tamari)		
Greens		
Boiled Salad - Umeboshi Dressing	10	15
Pickles		
Red Radish - Tamari	5	2hrs
Condiments		
Gomashio	(prepare ahead)	
Beverage		
Kukicha Tea		10
Dessert		

Brown Rice Boiled/Chick Peas
SHORT STEPS

1. Chick Peas - Soak overnight
2. Pickles
3. Chick Peas
4. Rice
5. Soup - Kombu stock
6. Nishime
7. Salad - prepare vegs
8. Chick Peas - tamari
9. Salad - cook
10. Soup - onions & carrots
11. Salad - make dressing
12. Soup - ginger & tamari
13. Soup - prepare scallions
14. Nishime - tamari
15. Tea

Good Food
> *Bad Food*
Foods that are good for you
> *Foods that are bad for you*
Is this a good food or is this a bad food?
There are so many different points of view.

But I do know that there are
Foods that are good for me and
> *foods that are bad for me.*
In most cases my body lets me know
> *Loud and Clear.*

But! do I eat the foods that I know are good for me
and avoid the foods that I know are bad for me?
Ah ha! Maybe that is the question,
> *and the answer.*

MENU

	Prep Minutes	Cooking Minutes
Soup		
Watercress Miso	5	20
(Wakame, onions, carrots, watercress, miso)		
Grain		
Millet Hash	30	90
1. Lentils (kombu, onions, carrots, lentils, tamari)	(10	60)
2. Millet (onions, cauliflower, parsnips, millet, salt)	(10	40)
3. Hash (onions, corn, carrots, broccoli stalks,	(15	20)
snow peas,oil, tamari, millet, lentils)		

Beans/Bean Products/Fish
(in millet hash)

Sea Veg
(in soup

	Prep Minutes	Cooking Minutes
Vegetables		
Sweet & Sour Red Cabbage	10	60
(red cabbage, tamari, mirin, umeboshi vinegar, rice syrup)		
Greens		
Collards	5	15
Pickles		
Carrots - Umeboshi Vinegar & Scallions	10	2 hrs

Condiments
Umeboshi Shiso Sprinkle   (purchased)

	Prep Minutes	Cooking Minutes
Beverage		
Kukicha Tea		10
Dessert		
Pumpkin Pie	60	60
1. Pumpkin, salt, agar	(15	20)
2. Couscous & granola	(10	10)

3. Pumpkin purée- pumpkin, tahini, soymilk,   (10   10)
   raisins, kuzu, barley malt, spices)
4. Bake Pie   (5   25)
5. Almond Purée (almonds, soymilk)   (10   )

Millet Hash with Lentils
SHORT STEPS

1. Hash - (1) lentils
2. Hash - (2) millet
3. Pickles
4. Dessert - (1) pumpkin
5. Hash - cook corn (use the cooking water in the soup)
6. Dessert - (2) couscous & granola
7. Dessert - (5) almonds
8. Soup - wakame, onions, carrots
9. Dessert - (3) pumpkin purée
10. Dessert - make pie shell and bake for 5 minutes
11. Vegetables
12. Dessert - fill pie and bake
13. Hash - (3) saute vegs
14. Hash - add lentils and millet
15. Soup - miso
16. Greens
17. Soup - watercress

GOOD GRIEF IT'S MONDAY ALREADY!

Do you dread Mondays?
Are they your Moandays?

Make them your Mydays.
Do something nice for yourself on Mondays.

MENU

	Prep Minutes	Cooking Minutes
Soup		
Leek Miso	10	20
(kombu, onions, carrots, leeks, miso)		
Grain		
1. Mashed Millet for Fish Cakes	(10	40)
(millet, onions, cauliflower,salt)		
Beans/Bean Products/Fish		
Fish Cakes	40	60
2. Onions, fish, tamari	(10	10)
3. Parsley	(5	)
4. Fish cakes	(15	15)
(mashed millet, onions & fish, parsley, flour, oil)		
Sea Veg		
Arame & Sunflower Seeds	10	30
(onions, carrots, arame, tamari, roasted sunflower seeds)		
Vegetables		
Baked Cabbage & Carrots	10	30
(cabbage, carrots, tamari, gomashio)		
Greens		
(in vegs)		
Pickles		
Grated Daikon - Tamari	10	2 hrs
Condiments		
Gomashio with Shiso	(prepare ahead)	
Beverage		
Dandelion Blend Ccoffee with Soymilk	10	

Dessert

Pumpkin Pudding (very light)   20   2 hrs
(pumpkin, tahini, raisins, cardamon, rice syrup, agar, kuzu,
vanilla)

Fish Cakes
SHORT STEPS

1. Dessert - Cut pumpkin, cook with salt, agar and water.
2. Millet - wash millet, cook with onions, cauliflower, salt, water.
3. Pickles - make and press pickles.
4. Fish - marinate in tamari and water.
5. Arame - soak for 5 minutes.
6. Veg - Shred cabbage, grate carrots. Bake with water, tamari and gomashio in a covered dish.
7. Arame - cut the onions and carrots.
8. Arame - cook with onions and carrots and water.
9. Dessert - purée pumpkin, add tahini, raisins, cardamon, rice syrup and vanilla. Return to heat. Add kuzu dissolved in cold water and stir until kuzu is cooked. Pour in cold dessert bowls and allow to set until thick. Can be refrigerated to speed up the setting.
10. Soup - kombu, onions, carrots and leek roots.
11. Fish cakes - sauté the onions and fish with water and tamari.
12. Fish cakes - chop parsley.
13. Fish cakes - mash millet, add fish, and parsley and form into patties. Roll in flour and fry in lightly oiled skillet.
14. Arame - add tamari (don't stir until ready to serve).
15. Soup - leek greens and miso.

The Lord does not look at the things man looks at.
Man looks at the outward appearance,
the Lord looks at the heart.
1 Samuel 16:7

MENU

	Prep Minutes	Cooking Minutes
Soup		
Light Miso	10	20
(wakame, onions, carrots, scallions, miso)		
Grain		
Mashed Millet to be used in Fish Loaf	10	40
(millet, onions, cauliflower, salt)		
Beans/Bean Products/Fish		
Fish Loaf	30	30
(whole wheat couscous, salt)		
(onions, fish, oil, tamari)		
(grated carrots, chopped onions)		
Sea Veg		
(in soup)		
Vegetables		
Cubed Turnips & Squash	10	20
(turnips, squash, salt)		
Greens		
Bok Choy	3	5
Pickles		
Grated Daikon - Tamari	10	2 hrs
Condiments		
Black gomashio	(prepare ahead)	
Beverage		
Dandelion Blend Coffee	5	
Dessert		
Apple Pie a la Difference	30	1 hr
Crust (whole wheat pastry flour, salt, oil, kinako)		
Bottom layer (apples, cinnamon, rice syrup, salt, flour)		
Middle layer (cranberries, rice syrup, kuzu)		

134

Top layer (raisins, walnuts, salt, kuzu)
Topping - Almond Whipped Cream
(almonds, vanila, soymilk)

Fish Loaf
SHORT STEPS

1. Fish Loaf - cook millet.
2. Dessert - make crust, roll out two crusts the size of the pie plate, place on cookie sheet and bake. Roll out bottom crust and place in the pie plate, top crust on waxed paper.
3. Dessert - cook cranberries, rice syrup and thicken with kuzu.
4. Dessert - cook raisins, walnuts, salt and thicken with kuzu.
5. Dessert - slice apples, toss with cinnamon, salt, rice syrup and flour and place in pie shell.
6. Dessert - place one baked layer on top of apples and add the cooked cranberries. Place second baked layer on top of cranberries and add raisins. Cover with top pie crust and bake.
7. Fish Loaf - cook couscous.
8. Fish Loaf - cook onions and fish.
9. Fish Loaf - grate carrots.
10. Fish Loaf - combine millet, couscous, fish and carrots. Place in lightly oiled loaf pan. Brush top with tamari, water and gomashio. Bake.
11. Vegs - cut and cook turnips.
12. Vegs - cut squash.
13. Dessert - make almond whipped cream.
14. Soup - wakame, onion and carrots.
15. Pickles - grate daikon and sprinkle with tamari.
16. Vegs - add squash.
17. Greens - bok choy.
18. Soup - miso.
19. Soup- scallions for garnish.

MENU

	Prep Minutes	Cooking Minutes
Soup		
Creamy Rice and Squash	15	3 hrs
(kombu, onions, rice, squash, tamari,parsley)		
Grain		
(in soup and dessert)		
Beans/Bean Products/Fish		
Chick Pea Patties	15	30
(parsnips, chick peas, onions, tahini, tamari)		
Sea Veg		
(in soup)		
Vegetables		
Boiled Salad - Tahini Dressing	25	15
(savoy cabbage, carrots, cauliflower, broccoli, onions)		
(tahini, umeboshi plum, parsley)		
Greens		
(in salad)		
Pickles		
Daikons - Sweet & Sour	5	2 hrs
(daikon, tamari, umeboshi vinegar, mirin)		
Condiments		
Gomashio	(prepare ahead)	
Beverage		
Dandelion Blend Coffee	5	
Dessert		
Millet Souffle	15	60
(millet, salt, raisins, vanilla, lemon rind, rice syrup, apples)		

Chick Pea Patties/Creamy Rice Soup
SHORT STEPS

1. Patties - Soak chick peas overnight.
2. Soup - Boil and simmer cooked rice.
3. Pickles - Cut daikon, add seasoning, press.
4. Dessert - Wash millet.
5. Dessert - Cook millet, raisins, lemon rind, salt and water.
6. Soup - Add kombu.
7. Soup - Cut onion fine and add.
8. Soup - Peel and cube squash and add.
** Soup - Stir occasionally.
9. Dessert - Slice apples.
10. Dessert - Mix apples with rice syrup, vanilla (cinnamon optional)
11. Dessert - Layer millet and apples in baking dish and bake 450° F for 20 to 40 minutes.
12. Patties - Blend chick peas, tahini and tamari in food processor but not to a smooth paste.
13. Patties - Grate parsnips.
14. Patties - Chop onions fine.
15. Patties - Mix chick peas, parsnips and onions and form into patties. Lightly coat with kinako.
16. Salad - Prepare all vegs.
17. Salad - Make dressing - tahini, umeboshi plum, water and parsley.
18. Salad - Cook vegs, one at a time in the same water, and place in serving bowl. As you place each veg in bowl, toss with dressing. Add the cabbage last but do not add more dressing.
19. Patties - Fry in lightly oiled skillet.
20. Soup - Tamari.
21. Soup - Chop parsley for garnish.

MENU

	Prep Minutes	Cooking Minutes
Soup		
Veggie Miso	15	20
(Wakame, onions, daikon, turnips, parsnips, carrots, cauliflower, broccoli, snow peas, miso, parsley)		
Grain		
Rice and Wheat	10	65
(rice, wheat, salt)		
Beans/Bean Products/Fish		
Seitan & Snow Peas in Onion Gravy	15	30
(seitan, onions, snow peas, tamari, kuzu)		
Sea Veg		
(in vegs)		
Vegetables		
Carrots, parsnips, broccoli, dulse	10	15
Greens		
(in vegs)		
Pickles		
Turnip - tamari	10	6 hrs +
Condiments		
Gomashio	(prepare ahead)	
Beverage		
Kukicha Tea		10
Dessert		
Apple Gingerbread	15	45
(whole wheat flour, dry soymilk,baking powder, ginger, cinnamon, cloves, barley malt, rice malt, oil, tahini, soymilk, apples,walnuts, raisins)		

Rice & Wheat / Seitan with Snow Peas
SHORT STEPS

1. Soak wheat 4 - 6 hours.
2. Turnip pickles - make at least 6 hours before using.
3. Rice and wheat
4. Dessert
5. Seitan - onions
6. Soup - wakame and onions
7. Soup - prepare all vegs
8. Seitan - seitan
9. Vegs - carrots and parsnips
10. Soup - all vegs except broccoli and snow peas
11. Seitan - tamari and kuzu
12. Vegs - broccoli
13. Soup - broccoli, snow peas, miso
14. Seitan - snow peas
15. Vegs - dulse
16. Soup - parsley garnish

Often during times of trouble we turn to prayer,
many times because we don't know what else to do.
Does praying get rid of the troubles?
Sometimes it does, depending on the trouble.
But there are troubles that we have to bear.
It is then that prayer gives us hope, courage, and strength
and the knowing that we are never alone
even during our worst moments.

MENU

	Prep Minutes	Cooking Minutes
Soup		
Ginger tamari	10	20
(kombu, onions, carrots, ginger, scallions)		
Grain		
Rice and arame	15	60
(rice, arame, roasted sunflower seeds, salt)		
Beans/Bean Products/Fish		
Tofu Cutlets - Natto miso sauce	15	20
(tofu, natto miso, tahini, umeboshi vinegar)		
Sea Veg		
(in grain)		
Vegetables		
1/ Burdock Kinpira	10	30
(onions, burdock, carrots, oil, tamari)		
2/Carrots	10	10
Greens		
Bok Choy	3	5
Pickles		
Mixed - tamari	10	2 hrs
(carrots, onion, cauliflower, broccoli, tamari)		
Condiments		
Gomashio - shiso leaves	(prepare ahead)	
Beverage		
Dandelion Blend coffee	5	
Dessert		
Quinoa Noodle Pudding	20	30
(noodles, apples, raisins, sunflower seeds,		
vanilla soymilk, tahini, ginger)		

MENU

	Prep Minutes	Cooking Minutes
Soup		
Veggie Miso	15	30
(wakame, onions, carrots, corn, cauliflower, broccoli, miso)		
Grain		
Brown Rice and Roasted Barley	15	60
(rice, barley, salt)		
Beans/Bean Products/Fish		
Split Peas	10	60
(split peas, onions, carrots, tamari, parsley)		
Sea Veg		
Hiziki	30	45
(hiziki, onions, roasted sunflower seeds, ginger, tamari)		
Vegetables		
Cauliflower and Broccoli	10	10
Greens		
(in vegs)		
Pickles		
Carrots - Tamari	5	2 hrs
Condiments		
Dulse Powder	(prepare ahead)	
Beverage		
Roasted Barley Tea		15
Dessert		

MENU

	Prep Minutes	Cooking Minutes
Soup		
Grated Carrot and Watercress	10	20
(kombu, onions, carrots, watercress, tamari)		
Grain (soak lotus seeds 4 hrs)		
Rice and Lotus seeds	5	50
(rice, lotus seeds, salt)		
Beans/Bean Products/Fish		
Sweet and Sour Tempeh	10	60
(tempeh, onion, carrot, tamari, umeboshi vinegar, mirin, gomashio, ginger, scallion)		
Sea Veg		
(in soup)		
Vegetables		
Baked Whole Squash	5	60
(squash, oil)		
Greens		
Bok Choy	5	10
Pickles		
Daikon - Tamari	5	2 hrs
Condiments		
Gomashio	(prepare ahead)	
Beverage		
Kukicha Tea		10
Dessert		

MENU

	Prep Minutes	Cooking Minutes
Soup		
Veg Miso	15	30
(wakame, onions, carrots, miso, carrot greens)		
Grain		
Brown Rice and Parsley	5	60
(rice, salt, parsley)		
Beans/Bean Products/Fish		
Scrambled Tofu	35	30
(tofu, onions, carrots, tamari, gomashio, umeboshi vinegar, mirin, ginger)		
Sea Veg		
Hijiki and Sunflower Seeds	30	30
(hijiki, onion, carrot, tamari, roasted sunflower seeds)		
Vegetables		
Carrots	5	10
Greens		
Savoy cabbage	5	15
Pickles		
Mixed - Sweet and Sour	10	2 hrs
(carrot, daikon, cauliflower, broccoli, tamari, umeboshi vinegar, mirin)		
Condiments		
Gomashio	(prepare ahead)	
Beverage		
Dandelion Blend Coffee	5	
Dessert		

MENU

	Prep Minutes	Cooking Minutes
Soup		
Ginger Tamari with Grated Carrots	10	15
(Kombu, onion, carrots, ginger, tamari, scallions)		
Grain		
Pasta - Sesame Rice Spirals	5	15
(pasta, salt, parsley)		
Beans/Bean Products/Fish		
Sweet and Sour Tempeh	10	60
(tempeh, onion, carrots, tamari, umeboshi vinegar, barley malt, ginger, oil, scallions)		
Sea Veg		
Arame with Carrots and Onions	10	30
(onions, arame, carrots, tamari)		
Vegetables		
Carrots and Chinese Cabbage with Umeboshi Sauce	20	15
(carrots, cabbage, salt)		
(umeboshi plum or paste, gomashio)		
Greens		
(in vegs)		
Pickles		
Mixed - Tamari	10	2 hrs
Condiments		
Ume Shiso Sprinkle	(purchased)	
Beverage		
Kukicha Tea		10
Dessert		

144

MENU

	Prep Minutes	Cooking Minutes
Soup		
Dulse, Squash	10	30
(onions, dulse, squash, miso, scallions)		
Grain		
Brown Rice and Black Soybeans	15	65
(rice, black soybeans, carrots, salt, parsley)		
Beans/Bean Products/Fish		
(in grain)		
Sea Veg		
(in soup)		
Vegetables		
Mashed Turnips and Squash	10	20
(turnips, squash, tamari, gomashio)		
Greens		
Kale	10	5
Pickles		
Daikon - Tamari	5	2 hrs
Condiments		
Gomashio	(prepare ahead)	
Beverage		
Dandelion Blend Coffee	5	
Dessert		

MENU

	Prep Minutes	Cooking Minutes
Soup		
Pumpkin Soup	15	30
(kombu, onions, pumpkin, ginger, tamari, parsley)		
Grain		
Noodles in Ginger Carrot Sauce	10	20
(noodles, salt) (carrots, ginger, tamari, kuzu)		
Beans/Bean Products/Fish		
Tofu Steak	10	20
(tofu, tamari, ginger, oil)		
(onions, mushrooms, carrots, scallions, tamari, mirin,		
umeboshi vinegar)		
Sea Veg		
(in soup)		
Vegetables		
Carrots and Snow Peas	10	10
Greens		
Romaine Lettuce and Carrot Curls - Pressed	10	60
(romaine, carrots, salt)		
Pickles		
Red Radish - Umeboshi Vinegar	10	2 hrs
Condiments		
Gomashio - Dulse	(prepare ahead)	
Beverage		
Kukicha Tea		10
Dessert		
Gingerbread with Apple Sauce	25	45
(whole wheat flour, dry soymilk, baking powder, ginger,		
cinnamon, cloves, barley malt, rice malt, oil, tahini, soymilk,		
raisins) (apples, salt, cinnamon)		

MENU

	Prep Minutes	Cooking Minutes
Soup		
Light Miso	10	20
(kombu, onions, carrots, miso, parsley)		
Grain		
Rice and Sesame Seeds	10	60
Beans/Bean Products/Fish	(soak beans overnight)	
Fava Beans	5	60
(fava beans, kombu, tamari)		
Cooked beans will be used in the stew.		
Sea Veg		
(Wakame - in stew)		
Vegetables		
Stew with Fava Beans	15	60
(onions, wakame, parsnips, turnips, carrots, squash, cauliflower, tamari)		
Greens		
Savoy cabbage	5	15
Biscuits		
Onion Biscuits	15	15
(w/w pastry flour, corn flour, salt, baking powder, oil, soymilk)		
Pickles		
Daikon - Tamari	10	2 hrs
Condiments		
Dulse	(prepare ahead)	
Beverage		
Kukicha Tea		10
Dessert		
Dandelion Blend Jell	5	30
(dandelion blend, carob soymilk, vanilla soymilk, agar, kuzu)		

147

MENU

	Prep Minutes	Cooking Minutes
Soup	(soak lotus root 3 hrs)	
Lotus Root - Tamari	15	30
(kombu, onions, lotus root, carrots, tamari, parsley)		
Grain		
Noodles - Linguine type		10
(noodles, salt)		
Beans/Bean Products/Fish		
Seafood Casserole	15	20
(onions, shitake, carrots, cauliflower, broccoli, snow peas, haddock, shrimp, scallops, soymilk, tamari, flour, scallions)		
Sea Veg		
(in soup)		
Vegetables		
(in casserole and salad)		
Greens		
Pressed salad	10	60
(romaine lettuce, boston lettuce,carrots, red cabbage, radishes, snow peas, salt)		
Pickles		
Grated Daikon - Tamari	10	2 hrs
Condiments		
Dulse	(prepare ahead)	
Beverage		
Dandelion Blend Coffee	5	
Dessert		
Apple Corncake	15	60
(whole wheat flour, cornmeal, baking powder, tahini, oil, barley malt, rice malt, vanilla soymilk, apples, raisins)		

MENU

	Prep Minutes	Cooking Minutes
Soup		
Grated Carrot Miso	10	20
(cooking water from noodles, kombu, onions, carrots, miso, parsley)		
Grain		
Lasagne Noodle Casserole.	45	45
1. Lasagne noodles, salt.		
2. Tempeh, onions, tamari.		
3. Squash, ginger, tamari.		
4. Homemade tofu cheese (make 2 days ahead).		
5. Monterey Jack tofu cheese (purchase).		
Beans/Bean Products/Fish		
(in casserole)		
Sea Veg		
(in soup and salad)		
Vegetables		
Greens		
Pressed Salad with Roasted Dulse	15	60
(romaine lettuce, carrots, salt, dulse)		
Pickles		
Sweet and Sour Mixed	10	2 hrs
Condiments		
Gomashio	(make ahead)	
Beverage		
Kukicha Tea		10
Dessert		
Rice Cookies	20	2 hrs
(rice, sweet rice, salt	5	45)
(rice syrup, currents, sunflower seeds	15	20)

MENU

	Prep Minutes	Cooking Minutes

Soup

Veggie Miso   10   20
(wakame, onions, daikon, squash, miso, parsley)

Grain

Pizza - Biscuit Pastry   45   45
1. Sauce - carrots, squash, ginger.
2. Whole wheat flour, oil, soymilk, kinako, baking powder, salt.
3. Onions, carrots, mushrooms, tofu weiners, tofu cheese.

Beans/Bean Products/Fish
(in pizza)

Sea Veg
(in soup)

Vegetables

Greens

Pressed salad   15   60
(red cabbage, umeboshi vinegar - blanch)
(romaine lettuce, carrots, radishes. blanched red cabbage, bean sprouts, umeboshi vinegar)

Pickles

Mixed Sweet and Sour   10   2 hrs
(onions, carrots, daikon, cauliflower, broccoli, tamari, umeboshi vinegar, mirin)

Condiments

Dulse   (prepare ahead)

Beverage

Kukicha tea   10

Dessert

Tahini Apple Custard   10   30
(apples, raisins, nuts, salt, rice syrup, tahini, cranberries, agar, kuzu, cinnamon)

Cooking the Whole Meal

Getting Ready to Cook

It is very important to relax and let go of the residue of the day before starting to prepare the meal. If you have been rushing all day, or feeling uptight, angry or frustrated, that is the energy that you put back in the food. You simply recycle the experiences of the day and feed these to your family. Much better to nourish yourself and your family with your own peace, love and joy. One of the easiest ways to let go of things and relax is by doing deep breathing. This is done standing and with the eyes closed. Inhale deeply through your nose and exhale slowly and completely through an open mouth with the sound of "ahhh". Do this five times. After the fifth breath, stand still for a few moments with the eyes closed. Then when you feel ready, smile, and looking downward, slowly and gently open your eyes.

Feel better?

Enjoy your cooking, enjoy your meal.

In the bonds of work I am free,
Because I am free from desire.
The man who can see this truth,
In his work he finds his freedom.
                    Bhagavad Gita 4:14

Brown Rice Pressure Cooked / Lentils

1. Pickles

1 medium onion
2 tsp tamari
2 tsp water
Pickle press or 2 bowls and weight

a) Peel onion and cut in thin wedges. This is known as the yin, yang cut: the expanded center (yin) and the contracted ends (yang). Using this cut you get part of the whole veg.
b) Place onion in pickle press.
c) Add 2 tsp water and 2 tsp tamari (tamari is natural soy sauce without sweeteners or additives).
d) Press for 2 hours. Onions can become bitter if pressed longer than two hours.
Onions can also be blanched before pressing, this takes away the sharp bite.

2. Rice

2 cups organic short grain brown rice
2 pinches sea salt
3 cups water
Large bowl, strainer, wooden paddle, pressure cooker

a) Wash rice in bowl and stir with wooden paddle. The dirt will float to the top. Drain off using strainer and repeat several times until the water is clear. If there are stones in the rice, it will be necessary to pick over carefully before washing. I prefer to use a wooden paddle when washing the rice as I find cold water on my hands is very painful and can be contracting for the kidneys.
b) Place rice in pressure cooker - add 2 pinches of salt (pinch of salt per cup of rice) and 3 cups of water (1 1/2 cups of water per cup of rice).
c) Cover the pressure cooker and place on high heat. Bring to full pressure and then lower heat and cook 45 - 50 minutes at

low pressure. When you become familiar with your pressure cooker you can bring rice to a boil then cover the pressure cooker but until you feel comfortable with the pressure cooker, it is safer to cover before placing on the heat. When the cooking time is up remove from heat and let pressure come down slowly. By cooking the rice at the beginning it frees up a burner that will be needed later. The rice will stay hot in the pressure cooker for 20 - 30 minutes.

3. Lentils

1 cup lentils	2" piece of kombu
1 medium carrot	1 - 2 tsp tamari
1 small onion	2 1/2 cups water
bowl, strainer, pot	

a) Break kombu into small pieces and gently wash. Place in bottom of pot. Use a small pot that is deep. I find that beans cook better if they are deep in a small pot rather than spread out in a large pot. Try both ways and see what you prefer.

b) Peel onions, cut in cubes about 1/2" and place on top of kombu.

c) Clean carrots, cut in small cubes about 1/2" and place on top of onions. (Another time use shaving method of cutting.) In Aveline Kushi's *Macrobiotic Cooking* she has a wonderful section on cutting carrots.

d) Carefully pick through lentils to remove stones and then gently wash. Place lentils on top of carrots.

e) Add the water slowly, pouring down the side of the pot so as not to disturb the vegs and lentils - about 3/4" of water over the top of the lentils. It might be necessary to add more water as they cook.
Bring to a boil, reduce heat and cook covered at a gentle simmer for about 40 minutes. Some types cook faster and others take much longer so I allow an hour to cook lentils. Lentils do not have to be soaked but for some people they are easier to digest if soaked.

Salt is not added until the lentils are 80% cooked. If salt is added too soon the lentils will not become soft. In this dish we will use tamari as the salting agent but it will be added in step 8.

Now check to see if the pressure is OK on the rice.
Remember also to check the lentils from time to time adding more water if needed. You want the lentils to be in a thick sauce, not dry or soupy.
Keep your work area neat and tidy as you cook. If there is clutter in your kitchen, there's clutter in your food and clutter in your life.

4. Soup

3" piece of kombu	*2 - 4 tps miso*
1" piece of daikon	*4 cups water*
1 med carrot	*soup pot*
1 small onion	

a) Break the kombu into very small pieces and gently wash to remove the dust and excess salt. If the kombu is well cooked it can also be eaten rather than just used to make soup stock. (For soup stock the whole piece would be used instead of breaking it up.)
   Put 4 cups of water in pot and add kombu, bring to boil and turn down to gentle simmer.

b) Slice onions very thin and add to soup. The longer onions cook the sweeter they become. If you want sweet tasting soup add onions at the beginning; if not add them nearer the end. Try both ways. Variety is what keeps this interesting.

c) Daikon takes a while to cook so slice it thin and add it now. (Daikon is a white radish and it helps to break down the animal fats stored in the body — your counsellor will advise you how often to have daikon).
   That's all we will add to the soup now, but will come back to it later. Soup can be cooked covered or uncovered.

5. Vegs - Carrots

4 medium carrots
pinch of salt
water
pot and steamer

a) Put about 1" of water in pot and bring to boil.
b) Clean and cut carrots. In this dish we will slice them on the diagonal. We will cook them when the water is boiling.

Check the other dishes that you have cooking on the stove.

6. Vegs - Broccoli

1 small head of broccoli
steamer

a) Wash broccoli and cut in flowerettes leaving about 3 - 4" stalk. Peel the remaining stalk if it's tough. Slice on the diagonal. The stalks will require more cooking time than the flowerettes. We will steam the broccoli after the carrots.

7. Soup

Slice the carrots paper thin. They will be added to the soup in the last 10 minutes (step 9).

8. Lentils

Check and taste the lentils - are they soft? Now add the tamari — not too much! You want the lentils to taste sweet not salty. This will now cook for another 10 - 20 minutes. If there is a lot of liquid you can now cook this uncovered so that it will cook down to a nice sauce.

9. Soup
Add the carrots.

10. Vegs
Is the water boiling? Put the carrots in a steamer and sprinkle with a pinch of salt. Steam for about 6 to 8 minutes covered.

11. Soup
Using a bowl or suribachi, purée the miso with soup water. Add to the soup and simmer 2 - 5 minutes.

12. Soup
Prepare parsley for garnish.

13. Kukicha Tea
Add about 2 tbsps twigs to 4 cups cold water. Bring to boil and gently simmer 8 - 10 minutes. Do not disgard the twigs after each meal, simply add more water and a few more twigs for the next cup of tea. Kukicha tea is very delicious — some people like it strong and some like it delicate. Experiment until it is just right for you.

14. Vegs
You can use a second stackable steamer on top of the carrots. Steam broccoli stalks first for 2 - 3 minutes. Then add the flowerettes and steam 2 - 3 minutes more or until they are at their peak of colour. (Experiment by watching a piece of broccoli cook: bright green is just right, dark and dull is overcooked).
It's by experimenting and tasting and watching that we learn. Many of us have burned rice and overcooked greens before we learned to get it just the way we like it.

It is important to stir rice before serving it to mix the yin/yang. The rice on top is softer, more yin while the rice on the bottom is harder, more yang. Dipping a wooden paddle in cold water before stirring prevents the rice from sticking to it.

I don't think I can stress variety enough — variety in foods and variety in cooking styles. If we do not have variety, even if we use only the best quality foods we will not get the balance we need. At the beginning it is difficult to know where to get all the nutrients we need, but by getting variety in our foods and cooking styles we will get a good balance.

The Basic Dietary Recommendations and *The Book of Macrobiotics* are good sources for nutritional value of foods.

Leftovers -
> Fried rice with lentils
> Lentil rice soup

Mashed Millet / Aduki Beans

1. Aduki beans
> *1 cup aduki beans*

Sort through beans and wash well. Soak overnight or at least 3 hours. It's really not necessary to soak aduki beans but it does make them easier to digest.

2. Pickles
> *2" piece of daikon*
> *2 - 3 tsp tamari*
> *2 - 3 tsp water*
> *pickle press or two bowls and a wieght*

Wash daikon with veggie brush or peel if not organic.
Cut diagonals about 1/8" thick and then cut in sticks. Place in pickle press, add tamari and water and press for 2 hours.

3. Aduki beans
> *3" piece kombu*   *1 - 2 tsp tamari*
> *soaked aduki beans*   *water*
> *1 onion*   *parsley - garnish*
> *1 cup squash*   *covered pot*

Wipe kombu to remove dust and excess salt. Place in bottom of pot. Slice onions and place on top of kombu. Add beans and just enough water to cover the beans. Bring to a boil uncovered. While waiting, wash, peel and cube the squash. Add squash to beans as soon as they come to a boil. Turn the heat down so they cook at a gentle, bubbling simmer and cover pot. Cook this way for 45 - 60 minutes adding cold water as needed. Tamari is not added until the beans are soft — about 80% cooked. To check to see if the beans are cooked cut a bean in half. The center, still uncooked, will be lighter in colour than the rest of the bean. When the bean is cooked completely it will be the same colour all the way through except for the skin.

4. Millet

2 cups millet	6 - 7 cups water
1 small onion	3 pinches sea salt
1 cup cauliflower	bowl
strainer and wooden paddle	
pot	

Peel and cube or dice onion and place in pot. Cut cauliflower in small flowerettes and place on top of onions. Wash millet in cold water using bowl and strainer. Stir with paddle and dirt will float to the top. Drain off and repeat several times until the water is clear. Add millet, salt and water to the pot. Place on medium heat and bring to a rolling boil. Reduce heat to low, cover and cook gently for 30 minutes.

5. Arame

1/2 cup arame	1 tsp tamari
1 small onion	1/2 cup water
1 small carrot	
bowl	small pot

Wash arame in cold water in bowl (the sand will settle to the bottom). Hold the arame up the side of the bowl and drain off the water and sand. Repeat once. Add a small amount of cold water to the arame and soak 5 minutes — this will make it possible to cut the arame.
Cut onion in thin half-moons and cover bottom of pot. Clean and cut carrots into sticks and place on top of onions.
Remove arame from water, place on cutting board and cut in 1" diagonals. Place arame on top of the carrots. Add enough cold water to just cover the onions and carrots, but not the arame. (If the arame is cooked in too much water the taste is much

stronger than when it steams on top of the onions and carrots. Bring to boil, reduce heat to low, cover and cook for 20 minutes. When cooking with small amounts of water it is a good idea to check periodically to ensure that it does not boil dry. We'll add the tamari in step 9.

6. Soup

1 3" strip kombu	1 small onion
1/2 cup watercress	2 - 3 tsp miso
4 cups water	pot

Wipe kombu, place in water and bring to boil. Lower heat and gently simmer for 10 minutes.
Slice onion paper-thin. This will be added in step 10.

7. Vegetables - preparation

1/4 medium buttercup squash
1 onion
1 tsp tamari
1 tbsp gomashio
covered skillet

Slice onions in wedges about 1/4" thick.
Wash and slice squash in 1/2" thick wedges. If squash is not organic it might be best to peel it.

8. Kale - preparation

4 big leaves kale	salt
water	pot

Wash kale in cold water (grubs love kale as much as we do and sometimes it is necessary to soak kale in salted water to get rid of this "extra protein"). Separate the leaves from the stem, tearing the leaves into 2 inch pieces. Slice the stems into thin diagonal pieces. Cook later.

9. Arame
Add about 1 tsp tamari to the arame and cook uncovered about 5 - 10 minutes, cooking off excess liquid. Do not stir yet. If this is stirred too soon the carrots will become quite dark. However they will retain their bright colour if stirred just before serving.

10. Soup
Remove kombu. This can be used in another dish. Add sliced onions and simmer 5 minutes.

11. Aduki beans
Check to see if almost cooked. If so, add tamari and cook for another 15 minutes. This may now be cooked uncovered if there is a lot of liquid. This should be saucy, not soupy.

12. Vegetables
In skillet combine water (about 1/2" deep), tamari and gomashio and bring to boil. Add onions and saute for 5 minutes. Place squash on top of onions, lower heat and simmer 10 - 15 minutes until squash is tender, adding more water if necessary. This can be cooked until the water has been absorbed or serve the cooking liquid as a sauce.

13. Kale
Put about 1" of water in pot and put on to boil.

14. Soup
Wash the watercress. Separate the leaves from the stems and cut the stems in small pieces. While it does, take a bit of time to remove the leaves rather than just chopping the leaves and stems. I really prefer seeing whole leaves floating in my soup — it is peaceful like lily pads on a pond. We will add the watercress later.

15. Soup
Purée the miso with a bit of soup water in a bowl or suribachi. Add to the soup, along with watercress and simmer 3 minutes. You can save some leaves to add as a garnish

16. Kale
Drop the kale stems in the boiling water and cook for about 5 minutes.

17. Millet
Mash the millet. Adding boiling water will make a softer consistency. A bit of ginger or gomashio will perk up the flavour. At the beginning many find that millet has a bland taste but after a short time the taste buds change and the flavor of millet is wonderful.

18. Kale
Add the kale leaves and cook for 2 or 3 minutes until they are bright green. Add a few grains of salt in the last minute. Place in a serving dish before you start eating your soup; otherwise they will overcook.

19. Coffee

Two Week Plan

Often when we see a counsellor we are advised to eat some foods daily, some 2 or 3 times a week and some weekly. Some foods are OK to have daily while others are best to have daily. Suddenly it is the end of the week, we still have a lot to eat and we have run out of meals.

A week at a glance menu takes care of that quite nicely. I normally do this on an 8 x 14 sheet of paper and I do 2 weeks at a time. In this way I can plan for what I like, include everything that I need and have lots of variety. The following is NOT a recommended weekly plan, but merely the format that I use. When planning the menu take into account your cooking time. While it is probably better to have the main meal at lunch time, for many this is not possible. It takes a bit of time to do the two week plan but it does save time and energy each day and sure takes the pressure off. Plan, cook, eat, enjoy!

	Monday	Tuesday
B R E A K F A S T	Miso Soup Kombu, onions, squash, miso, parsley - garnish Soft rice & barley porridge (use leftover rice and barley) Kukicha tea	Miso Soup wakame, onions, carrots, miso scallions - garnish Millet & squash Dandelion Blend coffee - *if using leftover millet cook squash separately*
L U N C H	Aduki bean soup (with rice and barley) Steamed greens Nori Tea -*soak lotus root for supper*	Soupy noodle dish with broccoli Nori Tea
S U P P E R	Miso Soup kombu, onions, daikon, carrots, miso, watercress garnish Smashed millet Fish Arame Lotus root in ginger miso sauce Carrots and tops Kale Grated daikon - tamari Gomashio Tea	Miso Soup wakame, onions, squash, miso watercress garnish Rice and black soybeans (dry roast black soybeans) Dried Daikon and kombu Nishime D Mixed greens Umeboshi plum Gomashio Coffee

	Wednesday	Thursday
B R E A K F A S T	Miso Soup Kombu, onions, turnip, miso, watercress - garnish Barley porridge Tea *- soak aduki beans*	Miso Soup Kombu, onions, parsnips, miso scallions - garnish Rice & raisins Coffee *- soak wheat for supper*
L U N C H	Rice and black soybean soup (onions and carrots) Boiled Salad Nori Tea	Millet hash Broccoli Nori Coffee
S U P P E R	Miso Soup kombu, onions,carrots, miso watercress - garnish Smashed millet (onions, carrots and parsnips) Auduki beans - kombu, onions, squash Hijiki Burdock kinpira Turnips and squash Collards Mixed brine pickles Tekka Tea	Miso soup wakame, onions, squash, miso parsley - garnish Rice & wheat Scrambled tofu Arame Carrots & tops Kale Daikon - tamari pickles Shiso Coffee *- make barley porridge, extra* *for soup on Saturday*

	Friday	Saturday
B R E A K F A S T	Miso Soup Wakame, onions, carrots, miso parsley - garnish Barley porridge with sunflower seeds Coffee	Miso Soup Kombu, onions, squash, miso watercress - garnish Rice and umeboshi Tea
L U N C H	Noodles in sweet veg sauce Boiled Salad Nori Tea	Barley soup or stew Chinese cabbage & ume vinegar Nori Tea - *soak lotus root*
S U P P E R	Miso Soup kombu, onions, carrots, miso scallions - garnish Rice Veg stew with tempeh & cabbage Dried daikon & kombu Watercress Takuan pickles Sea veg condiment Tea	Miso Soup wakame, onions, turnips, miso scallions - garnish Smashed millet with squash Aduki beans, kombu, onions, squash Nishime B Kale Mixed tamari pickles Gomashio Tea or coffee

Sunday

B R E A K F A S T	Miso Soup Wakame, onions, carrots, miso parsley - garnish Millet & quinoa porridge Pureed squash Coffee
L U N C H	Dulse, squash & split pea soup Rice cakes Steamed greens Nori Tea
S U P P E R	Miso Soup kombu, onions, carrots, miso parsley - garnish Rice (grated carrots & ume shiso) Fish Hijiki & sunflower seeds Burdock kinpira Carrots, cauliflower, snow peas (treat) Bok Choy Grated Daikon - tamari Gomashio Tea

Several years ago, while working on a project, a friend and I decided that we needed a guideline so we wrote up our Seven Steps. While these particular steps will not apply to everyone, I encourage anyone on a healing regime to write up their own steps to help them focus on their own needs.

The Great Life - Seven Steps

1. We acknowledge that we have a burning desire to live and we accept that proper diet, our lifestyle, exercise, gratitude, love and God are essentials for harmony.

2. We realize that all of our sickness and unhappiness have resulted from nothing but our own fears, mistakes, improper judgement and lack of gratitude. We resolve to change and we can turn our direction into one of continuing health and happiness.

3. We realize that to live happily and in good health we have to live TODAY with awareness: yesterday is past and tomorrow will look after itself.

4. We realize that in order to achieve harmony (health, happiness and inner peace) we will also experience dis-harmony (dis-ease, dis-comforts and disturbances).

5. We realize that we have to love ourselves, love our fellow men and love God. They are all one and the same; to love any one of these is to love all three. We can start with any one of these.

6. There is love and there is fear; we choose love.

7. We acknowledge that the support, love and guidance that we receive from family, friends and God has a tremendous impact on our own improvement and healing and we will continually support others in the best way we can.

Books

The following books have been very useful to me on my healing journey, not only as a source of information but also as a source of guidance and inspiration. When I started macrobiotics I had difficulty finding cookbooks in my area. However, there were many wonderful cookbooks written in the 1980's which are available in all good health food stores. I really enjoy cookbooks and whenever I get a new one I read it from cover to cover.

Macrobiotic Dietary Recommendations - Michio & Aveline Kushi

The Book of Macrobiotics - Michio Kushi

The Cancer Prevention Diet - Mushio Kushi

The Macrobiotic Way - Michio Kushi

Macrobiotic Diet - Michio and Aveline Kushi

The Book of Do-In - Michio Kushi

Macrobiotic Home Remedies- Michio Kushi

Diabetes and Hypoglycemia - Michio Kushi

Cooking for Health Diabetes and Hypoglycemia - Aveline Kushi
     (there are other books in this education series)

Macrobiotic Cooking - Aveline Kushi

Healing Ourselves - Naboru Muramoto

Food and Healing - Annemarie Colbin

The Natural Gourmet - Annemare Colbin

Natural Foods Cookbook - Mary Estella

Uprisings - The Whole Grain Bakers' Book

Practically Macrobiotic - Keith Mitchell

The Self-Healing Cookbook - Kristina Turner

The Cure is In the Kitchen - Sherry A. Rogers

I am grateful to Aveline and Michio Kushi and all the other authors who have put so much loving energy into their work.

Glossary

Aduki (or Azuki) Beans
Small, dark red bean.

Agar agar
Gelatin from sea vegetable.

Arame
Black noodle-like sea vegetable.

Arrowroot Flour
Starch flour used as a thickener.

Barley
Whole cereal grain.

Barley Malt
Natural sweetner made from barley. Dark in colour and has a rich strong taste.

Black Soybeans
Also called Japanese black beans.

Brown Rice
Whole rice unpolished.

Bulgar
Whole wheat, cracked, partially boiled and dried.

Burdock
The plant that burrs grow on. The root is used in cooking.

Couscous
Cracked wheat that has been partly refined.

Daikon
White radish. Also know as lobok.

Dandelion Blend
Coffee made from dandelion roots, barley and rye. Caffeine free.

Dulse
Reddish sea vegetable.

Fava Beans
Like broad beans.

Ginger
Root used in cooking for its spicy pungent taste. Also used medicinally.

Gomashio
Condiment made from sesame seeds and sea salt.

Hijiki
Sea vegetable, much like arame only coarser.

Kelp
Sea vegetable used in soups and stews, much like kombu.

Kinako
Roasted soybean flour.

Kombu
Sea vegetable used in soups, beans dishes and stews.

Kukicha Tea
Tea made from the twigs of the Japanese tea bush. Contains little caffeine.

Kuzu
White starch used as a thickener, much like arrowroot but also has medicinal qualities.

Lentils
Small, flat green or brown bean.

Lotus Root
Root of the water lily. Used for its delicious taste and also its medi-inal value.

Lotus Seeds or nuts
From the water lily plant. The size and shape of chickpeas, they have a smoky, nutty taste.

Millet
Small, yellow grain. Cooked whole or in combination with other foods. (Used in birdseed) .

Mirin
Sweet cooking wine made from sweet rice.

Miso
Known also as soybean paste. Fermented and aged. Made from soybeans, salt and another grain or bean.

Natto Miso
Condiment made from shortly fermented soybeans, grain and ginger.

Nishime
Style of cooking like braising.

Nori
Sea vegetable used in sushi, or toasted and served as is.

Oat Groats
Whole oats, used in porridge.

Quinoa
Small grain high in protein.

Rice Syrup or Malt
Natural sweetner made from brown rice.

Sea Peas
Delicious green plant that grows wild along the seacoast.

Seitan
Wheat gluten or wheat meat. Used in cooking soups, stew, burgers, tourtiere, etc.

Shiso Leaves
Beefsteak leaves, pickled and used in condiments.

Shitake Mushrooms
Japanese mushrooms. Normally used dried in cooking or for medicinal uses.

Soymilk
Liquid from making tofu.

Sweet Brown Rice
Sweet, glutinous rice.

Tahini
Paste made from ground sesame seeds.

Tamari
Natural soy sauce.

Tempeh
Fermented soybean product used as a meat replacement in cooking.

Tofu
Soybean curd. High in protein, use widely in cooking, from meat replacement to ice cream replacement.

Ume Shiso Sprinkle
Condiment made from umeboshi plums and shiso leaves.

Umeboshi Plum
Salty, pickled, aged plum used in cooking, condiments and for its medicinal value.

Umeboshi Vinegar or Ume-su
The liquid that umeboshi plums are aged in. Used in cooking sauces, dressing, pickles, etc.

Wakame
Sea vegetable, like kombu, that is used in soups.

Index